Dialogues
About
Adoption

Conversations Between
Parents and Their Children

Linda Bothun

 Swan Publications

Library of Congress Catalog Card Number: 94-69688
ISBN 0-9619559-1-0

10 9 8 7 6 5 4 3 2 1

Swan Publications
P.O. Box 15293
Chevy Chase, Maryland 20825
202-244-9092

To Ana and Jonathan, my dual inspirations, to Dave who endured my windows battle, to Erving and Lela and Vi who are always supportive, and to Jan Nagel Clarkson, my editor and friend, and without whom *Dialogues* wouldn't be ... thanks and love.

This book is dedicated
to
The Moms Group
that helped me keep perspective.

I offer one of my favorite vignettes to these moms:

Elizabeth was recounting her family's excitement upon first seeing their two-year-old daughter at the orphanage in Colombia.

Gillian interrupted, "Let me get this straight. You adopted your son as a three-year-old, and now, two years later, you've just adopted a two-year-old? How brave of you!" There was admiration touched with skepticism in her tone.

"Anyone," Elizabeth replied, "anyone who decides to become a parent takes a risk."

Contents

Prologue

"I heard a lecture about adoption months ago that is still bothering me. Or one word is," a young father of an 18-month-old boy began. "The speaker, who was excellent, commented that we must remember—adoption is 'different.' He didn't elaborate, and I don't understand. Aren't we to think of ourselves as normal?" he asked poignantly.

❖

As a writer and adoptive parent, I began to wonder if "different" is a wise choice of words to use to describe a family which has been built through adoption. This father had interpreted the word "different" to mean "abnormal."

But a look at the dictionary left me thinking the word "different" is fine. It means "partly or totally unlike" and "dissimilar." Adoptive parents realize that adoption is partly unlike or dissimilar from having a child born into the family or they wouldn't strive to learn how best to handle the questions that arise from the "differences." The answer seems to be that while adoption is in fact "different," the term is not used pejoratively. A few other examples of situations where "different" is not "abnormal," but simply "different," might help.

In our world today, because of extensive travel and access to the media, we are acutely aware of cultural "differences." While we may prefer our own because of familiarity, we are certainly cognizant of the fact that few cultural practices are inherently better than any others. They are simply different, and if we are aware of the differences, we can understand and respect each other.

Some linguists assert that men and women have "different" conversational styles. That one is not better than the other. That they are simply "different." It is helpful to understand the conversational style of the opposite sex and it is helpful to understand our own. It assures us that these "differences" are okay and makes communication easier.

Saying adoption is "different" means that it is an issue and a reality that must not be ignored but must be handled as questions arise. Saying adoption is "different" means that our children have one additional issue to deal with as they face the often turbulent growing-up years—but only one more issue. Saying adoption is "different" means there are more children born into families than adopted into families, though with today's cacophony of life-styles, step families, single-parent families, and so forth, it is becoming increasingly difficult to define what *isn't* "different." And of course, each of these life-styles can be functional or dysfunctional, and isn't that after all what is important.

Perhaps there's a better word than "different," but I'm at a loss at the moment to say what it might be. I think the speaker was simply saying that we adoptive parents have been given one additional challenge in our parenting. I, for one, will gladly accept that responsibility for the privilege of being a family.

❖

Chapter One
About Dialogues

The crowded room was perfectly still. The proverbial pin dropped, but no one heard it, so intent was everyone on the unfolding story. It was a simple story, one of many told during the course of the evening, of what a child had asked and what a parent had answered. The subject was adoption.

Every parent leaned forward to hear the outcome, knowing that some-day he would be in a similar situation, and, oh, to handle it well was the desire in every heart.

The meeting ended, but the feeling within me would not go away—the feeling that these stories would be helpful to all adoptive parents.

And so the gathering for this book began. During the past three years, I have researched written material on the topic and have convened groups of parents and adoption agency personnel who shared experiences that could be included in this book. I have solicited contributions via news-letters and at workshops at which I have spoken. Some stories have been mailed to me or left on my answering machine. Others are from my own experience or have been reconstructed from informal conversa-tions over the years.

Names, settings, and circumstances have been altered so that no child will feel his confidences have been compromised. All dialogues are truthful and were said by loving parents who, often under duress, searched for the best responses, sometimes intuitively stumbled upon them, and sometimes didn't. All stories are shared with the hope that they will be of help to others.

You may find that you agree with how a particular exchange was handled, and you may not. If you disagree with what was said, feel fortunate that you have had the opportunity beforehand to think through your own response. These parents didn't. A profound question or comment can and will be thrust upon an adoptive parent when least expected: loudly in a long line at the grocery store, quietly and confidentially when the light has been turned low and the bedtime story is just finished, in the carpool with five other sets of curious ears listening.

The best assurance that you will be able to handle these questions well when they arise seems to be forethought. If you're aware that the queries will probably come, if you're aware of how other people have dealt with them, then your choice of answer may come more easily to you.

In many discussions about adoption, there's not necessarily a right or a wrong response. You know your child and the nuances of his particular line of questioning. But countless adoptive parents have been grateful to have known some of the conversations that have taken place between other parents and children. They have built on them or altered them as the situation has required, but most importantly, they've not been surprised by the questioning. They have been able to sit back and in essence say, "Oh, here comes the 'do I really belong' question."

And without feeling threatened or somehow personally at risk, they have been able to deal with the issue at hand, knowing it's a perfectly normal developmental line of reasoning for a child who was adopted, thankful that the child has had the confidence to talk about it, knowing how various people have answered the questions, and knowing that, if they are kind and truthful, they are on the right track.

Sometimes parents feel unsettled if they haven't "wrapped up" a conversation about adoption, concluded it, found a resolution. The truth is that many of these issues are not resolvable. There may likely be no "pat" answer that satisfies everyone.

In fact, "wrapping it up," especially in an "I'll make it all better" sense, may be more harmful than helpful. These are big and important and consequential issues, and as with all such issues, even in the adult world, there are usually no easy answers, and often no answers at all. Voicing them is the important thing, and eventually a person, a child in this case, can come to live with them and accept them on some level or find a way to do something about them.

Occasionally, a parent will feel the need to "buy time" when the child has asked an important question. Saying "That's an interesting question, and I want to take time to think about it" will give the parent a chance to discuss it with a friend or spouse. This response might even give the child a chance to give additional thought to the issue, and the ensuing discussion may be more meaningful when the parent brings it up at a later time.

The important thing to remember is that simply *having* the conversation is valuable. The concern has been aired. The unspoken feeling on the part of the child may be, "At least I have been listened to and taken seriously. I guess there's no real answer, but at least someone knows how I feel."

An overriding precaution when answering children's questions about adoption is the adage: Answer the question , answer it truthfully, but don't tell more than is asked at that particular time. If the next question is asked, answer it of course.

The instructive joke regarding talking with children about sex applies equally well when talking with children about adoption. In addition to resisting the urge to "tell the whole story" about adoption at one time, adoptive parents need to listen carefully to the question their child asks before they answer. Remember the little girl who asked her mother, "What does sex mean?" She listened patiently to her mother's explanation and then rejoined, "But, Mommy, I meant on this form. What is sex? Am I an M or an F?"

A note of caution, then. After reading this book, parents will have at their disposal a number of approaches to questions. It is probably not wise to answer a question on any given subject in its entirety as presented on these pages. Your child may be asking just half of the question at that particular moment. In that case, he should receive the answer only to what he has asked. He will ask for more if he is ready to handle more.

There is a converse side to this caution, too. Some parents of older children admit frustration when they read these vignettes or hear similar ones. They say, "Johnny (it's usually a boy) is 11 and he never asks any questions. He never has." Parents voicing this concern are usually worried that they've done something wrong. They say they've been open and available, but that their child just hasn't asked.

And that is often simply a matter of personality. Some children are more inquisitive than others. Some talk constantly about everything. Some talk only about those things that don't touch their emotions. Some have gained understanding in ways parents are unaware. Some will talk later. Some never. If it is a serious concern, parents can consult with a counselor who is experienced in dealing with children who were adopted, someone who can either calm their fears or help them decide how to proceed.

Some children, on the other hand, are ready to talk, or at least to listen. An appropriate book can be presented to a child with the simple explanation that "some kids who were adopted like to read this book when they're your age." Videos and cassettes that deal with various aspects of adoption can be purchased. Be sure you agree with the approach of the cassette before presenting it to your child!

Another non-threatening suggestion for broaching subjects that parents intuitively feel may be troubling their children, or are at least of some concern to them, is to open the subject at an opportune time with a generalization which removes the personal aspect. For example, "Some kids, around their birthdays, start thinking about what is was like when they were born." At times this is enough to prompt the child to continue the conversation. Often it isn't. In fact, a more reticent child may forcefully retort, "Well, *not me!*" If the response is a bit too adamant, you just may have guessed right! At that point, a few more well-chosen sentences are usually helpful. Parents need to remember that a child can be absorbing information and may even be extremely grateful for the one-sided conversation, but may never tell the parent so.

Certainly this technique should not be overused and must be carefully balanced with "the urge to tell the whole story," but a parental hunch is often correct. The child may have been giving clues or the parent may be aware that, developmentally, the child is probably having thoughts along those lines. The child may be eager for the information or at least he may be comforted to know that the subject is within limits. If it's not appropriate for him, he will shrug it off, and if the exchange has been casual enough, undoubtedly no harm has been done.

Each chapter of this book is introduced with examples of generally accepted developmental information. Dialogues within each chapter have been placed chronologically based on the age of the child when that conversation took place. Certainly a dialogue about any subject can happen when a child is at a different age or stage in his development.

Some of the stories come out picture perfect. Some don't. Some reach nice conclusions with everyone satisfied. Some don't. All are valuable to adoptive parents who will probably find themselves, eventually, in conversations identical to or much like these. Each vignette recounted here simply tells one true story.

Chapter Two

Telling The Story

The first vignettes in this book are those which contain some facet of "telling the story," telling the child the story of his adoption.

As parents read these conversations experienced by other adoptive parents and their children, it is important for them to keep in mind all they know about developmental stages of children—all children—adopted or born into their families. For a feeling or emotion evidenced by a child who was adopted needs to be looked at in the larger context of child development as a whole. A seven-year-old might be extremely positive about his adoption at one moment and extremely negative about it the next, and might be moody and sulking at times, but seven-year-olds, generally, *are* extremely positive one moment and extremely negative the next, and *are* moody and sulky, adopted or not.

Keeping in mind the normal developmental stages, agreed upon by most child development experts, can help parents remember that their children are going through perfectly normal stages—with the additional issue of adoption on their minds.

Commonly the preschool child, for example, will embrace his adoption story, often heralding the tale as he will any other unusual tidbit of family lore. It's usually okay with the preschooler to be different, unique. In fact, it's exciting. Let's tell everyone!

The school-aged child, now able to understand adoption and all else at a deeper level, may rather suddenly dislike the fact that he was adopted, for this is the time when children generally don't want to be different from their peers in any way. Question upon question often tumbles out during these years, and his adoption simply may not feel okay to the child until he can understand and accept the facts on a new level.

While some adolescents indeed sail through this time of changing bodies and changing needs in terms of independence, some young people find the going difficult. If in fact his life seems imperfect to him, as do the lives of many adolescents, the one who was adopted has a handy "reason" for his unhappiness. The adolescent born to his family will simply have to be more creative in determining a whipping post!

Parents' awareness of this developmental phase does not negate in any way the importance of dealing with issues. However, it is imperative for all parents to remember that the adolescent, adopted or born into his family, often needs to find something to kick against in order to establish independence. With that perspective, adoptive parents can deal with the situation at hand, aware of its normalcy, not concerned that it displays pathology, and consequently feel secure enough to follow their parental instincts as should any caring parent.

Conventional wisdom has changed over the years as to if or when or how to tell a child about his adoption. Currently, it is commonly held that a child "should not remember a time when he didn't know." And so most often today the story is told, simply and early, insuring that the child first hears of his adoption from his parents.

The first of the dialogues is an example of the story that was repeated with various nuances by dozens of parents who were interviewed. While some parents feel the story should begin with happenings prior to the actual adoption, these parents began with the part they knew best: their own feelings and the simplest version of their child coming into their lives.

❖

Taylor and Todd: ages two and three

Taylor had loved "little lamb" stories since she was tiny. Her mother Kathryn would concoct a lengthy bedtime story each evening, a story whose star was a little lamb who had always had a day pretty much like Taylor's, it turned out.

When Taylor's little brother, Todd, was born into their family, the bedtime stories grew to encompass the activities of two little lambs. It was natural, then, that the adoption and birth stories be told using those same little creatures.

"And one day the mommy lamb and the daddy lamb decided they wanted a baby lamb," Kathryn said to her daughter who was too young to be concerned about the plausibility of that statement. "And so they went to the adoption agency where they were presented with a baby lamb that needed a home. And then they wanted another baby lamb, and so the mommy lamb went to the hospital where a baby lamb was born to her. And then the mommy lamb and the daddy lamb were *so* happy, because they had a daughter and a son whom they loved so much."

Kathryn told this story, sometimes embellished, every two or three weeks until Taylor and Todd were two and three years old. And then the day came when they were all at the kitchen table, and the time seemed right for additional information.

"Remember the little lambs that we talk about before we go to sleep?" Taylor and Todd nodded enthusiastically as Kathryn continued. "Who do you think those little lambs are, really?" she asked.

It was a new puzzle, and of course Taylor and Todd knew the answer. They pointed to themselves.

"Right!" Kathryn and her husband Rick cheered. "Now, who is the little lamb that was adopted into our family?"

"Right!" they cheered again as Taylor proudly pointed both index fingers at herself.

"And who is the little lamb that was born into our family?"

"Right!" Another cheer as Todd guessed who.

"More will come later, much more. But now our children have heard about adoption and birth from their father and me," Kathryn said. "They won't be surprised and confused by hearing about it from someone else first."

From then on Kathryn and Rick would talk about the subject only occasionally and wait for questions from their children. But here they felt they had begun a foundation for the understanding that they would build on as the years went by.

❖

Zach: age three

Zach was three the year Zoe came to the Jamisons. Nancy happened that year to be chairperson of the large fund-raising auction that parents put on for their agency.

Chairing the auction was a big job, and poor Zach probably heard more about it than he cared to. Nancy lived and breathed "auction," people came to their house regularly bearing boxes and folders, and so you can see Zach's confusion when Zoe arrived. He was sure the Jamisons had gotten her at the auction!

"No, Zach, we didn't get Zoe at the auction. It's not quite like that," Nancy chuckled to herself.

The Jamisons decided to get a babysitter for Zoe and take Zach to the hotel on the day of the event so that his three-year-old mind could separate these two events. He didn't understand "auction" any more than he understood "adoption," but his parents provided as much reality for him as was possible.

❖

Sally: age four

Sally was nearly four, and Lynn and John felt quite comfortable with the amount of information they had given her about her adoption and with the number of times they had brought up the subject. They wanted her "never to remember a time when she didn't know," as they had been advised, but they also, in their own words, didn't want to "rub her nose in it."

The lady at the mall probably didn't even catch the nuance of Sally's question, and she certainly wasn't offended, but Lynn and John had a good laugh later about Sally's little chat that afternoon. She had gone up to a sweet-looking mom pushing her infant in a carriage and had asked, "Where did you get your baby?"

Evidently they'd not quite made clear to Sally that not *all* children are adopted.

❖

Stacy: age four

Helen had taken the opportunity of her friend's pregnancy to explain a bit about the birth process to her four-year-old daughter, Stacy, who had been adopted as an infant. Stacy and her friend Emmy, the proud big sister-to-be, had been allowed to feel the baby kick that morning, and, fascinated, Stacy had asked questions intermittently throughout the day.

Finally the inevitable question came, the one Helen had anticipated. "Mommy, did I grow in your tummy?"

"No, sweetheart, you didn't grow in my tummy."

There was a long silence, and Helen thought that might be the end for that day. But Stacy finally continued. "But where did I grow?"

"You grew in the tummy of another woman, sweetie. And then Daddy and I adopted you. So another woman gave birth to you, but now Daddy and I are your parents forever and ever."

Helen waited for the "Why?" and "Who?" questions, but they didn't come that day. She knew they would come later, and they would be answered just as truthfully at that time.

❖

Alexandra: age five

Alexandra was only five, but she had her succinct explanation ready for her friends. She hadn't been asked, but she had decided to bestow her short lecture on her kindergarten class one day.

"My birthmother was a teen like my babysitter. She could grow me inside her, but she couldn't be a parent. And my mommy couldn't grow me inside her, but she could be a parent."

❖

Jimmy: age five

When the Lowens first child arrived, their neighbor ran over to offer her congratulations. She, too, had adopted her children, and she understood their excitement.

She had one story to laughingly relate. "We emphasized the positive about adoption to our children," she said. "Actually, we must have *overemphasized* the positive."

The principal, it seems, had called her at the end of her oldest son Jimmy's first day at school. "I wondered if you could help," he began. "Jimmy is making the other children in his class feel bad."

Jimmy had spent the day announcing, "My parents picked me out. Your parents had to take what they got!"

❖

Mary Ellen: age five

At their family gathering in small-town Wisconsin, five-year-old Mary Ellen overheard her uncle telling his son, "That's the hospital where I was born." Mary Ellen's mother Miriam added to her daughter, "Your daddy was born there, too, honey."

After a moment's thought, Mary Ellen asked, "Where was I born, Mommy?"

Miriam responded, "Remember, honey, Daddy and I first saw you at the agency when we adopted you. We don't know where you were born."

A brooding silence followed. Miriam wished she'd said it differently.

"I'm quite sure all my daughter needed at that point was for me to say, 'Oh, you were born in a hospital, too, but a larger one than this,' a truthful statement because we knew only that it was a large suburban hospital," Miriam said.

"If Mary Ellen had asked *which* hospital, something I think did not matter to her at her age, I could have said we didn't know. But I had inadvertently made her feel more 'different' than she needed to feel at that time."

14

Catherine: age six

The minister had just begun the long communion prayers when Lenore's six-year-old daughter Catherine whispered, "Mom, did I come from an orphanage?"

Lenore gulped. "No. Why do you ask?"

"Thea's mom told her that I was in an orphanage," Catherine said.

"Well," Lenore said, "you weren't in an orphanage. After you were born, you were taken care of by a woman named Sue and then we met you and you came to live with us. So you were always with people who cared about you."

Silence. Lenore felt she hadn't done a good job. Then she remembered "the plan."

At the next break, Lenore whispered, "Orphanages are for children whose birthmothers couldn't make any plans for them. Maybe the birthmothers died or something. That didn't happen for you. The woman who grew you made a plan for you. She was careful that you would have a good family to love you. She made sure you would always have someone to take care of you. You never were in an orphanage."

"Are orphanages bad places?" was the next question.

"Well," Lenore said, every negative cliche in the world looming before her, "there are good ones and bad ones. Pippi Longstocking was in a bad one. And remember Annie in the movie? Hers was bad, too. But remember our friend Ana? She was from an orphanage in Colombia, and I've seen pictures of it. It was beautiful, with lots of people to care for the children, and lots of love and laughter."

Lenore couldn't tell if she'd said the right things or not, but Catherine put her head in her mother's lap. As Lenore stroked her daughter's hair, Catherine seemed relaxed and at peace.

❖

Darby: age six

It had been several weeks since she and her mother had had a conversation about adoption, but obviously the subject was on six-year-old Darby's mind. She had put her crayons down and was just sitting at the kitchen table, looking dreamily out the window when she said to no one in particular, "I was three weeks old when I came home...."

❖

Alan and Hannah: ages seven and three

The Zellar family had spent a quiet evening reading books, one of which was a story about why and how a baby was adopted into a family. They occasionally read something that they hoped would stimulate thinking and talking about adoption, knowing that this issue needed to be talked about over and over and that the understanding would happen in stages. On this particular evening, their children wanted to talk.

"Why don't we get another baby?" Alan, age seven, wondered, with three-year-old Hannah nodding in agreement.

"Well, it's hard," Dan responded. "We feel so lucky that we have two children. It would be so much fun to have three, but then our agency is worried that some other family might not get to have a child."

The children were already in bed, and it was getting quite late for any additional lengthy discussion, and so Terri and Dan just smiled at each other at Alan's eventual response. "Well, Mom, why don't you just get pregnant?"

The children had absorbed the story that had just been read to them at some level, but they had missed one of the finer points! Another time, another story, and they would gradually understand. The Zellars knew the children would grasp more when they were more mature, when they were able to think more abstractly.

❖

Rebecca: age seven

"Why did I have to be adopted? I don't like adopted!" seven-year-old Rebecca said adamantly. "Why did she let me be adopted?"

"I can understand how you feel, honey," her mother Marie gently responded. "You love your mommy and daddy, and yet you wonder about your birthmother and wish things could have been different."

This seemed to assure Rebecca of her mother's acceptance of her feelings and gave her permission to continue. "Why did she do it? Why did she give me away?" she stormed. "Was I so ugly?" was the ironic question from the lips of one of the most beautiful little girls that Marie had ever seen.

"Oh, honey, no, no, no! You were a beautiful, beautiful baby, and you were such a wonderfully easy baby to care for. Do you know that you slept through the entire night the first night you were here with Daddy and me? You slept from 11 p.m. until 7 a.m., and believe me, most babies don't do that.

"No, honey, it had *nothing* to do with you. You were a perfect baby. The woman who gave birth to you simply wasn't ready to be a mom at that time. She was very young and she thought she should finish high school. She just didn't think it would be a very good life for either of you just then. '

"Kind of like she was a girl herself?" Rebecca asked, partially quoting a line she and her mother had read together recently in a children's book about adoption.

"That's right."

"Do you think she cried?"

"I'm positive she did, even though I never talked to her. It must have been the hardest thing she'd ever done."

"I hope she's okay. I think about her sometimes."

"I think about her sometimes, too. I'll always be grateful to her, grateful that Daddy and I have you."

"Mom?"

"Um-hum?"

"I'm so glad you chose me."

They hadn't gotten to choose their daughter. That's not exactly the way adoption happens. But Marie decided not, at that precious moment, to correct Rebecca's minor misconception.

❖

Whitney: age seven

Ellen was surprised at the emotion she was feeling after her conversation with her daughter.

It had not been particularly easy. Whitney, seven, had made it abundantly clear that it no longer felt all right to her to be adopted. Ellen knew this was the beginning of the age when children don't want to be "different" in any way from other children. While Whitney had always cheerfully chattered about adoption in the past, this morning she had crossly insisted, "You're not my real mommy. I wish she could raise me."

Ellen was ready for the possible exchange, and her voice was calm and understanding and reassuring. The words had come rather easily. Ellen knew not to feel personally threatened by her daughter's feelings. But the emotion that was there instead was unexpected.

Relief. It was relief. Not relief that it was over, but relief that the conversation had happened at all.

The realization flooded over Ellen. Whitney had been able to speak her mind and express her feelings not because she felt insecure, but because she felt secure! So sure was she of her mother's love that she could chance saying those things that were occurring to her as she began the stage of abstract thinking and began to understand adoption on another level.

"Here we go," thought Ellen, knowing this was only the beginning of the dialogue. And she felt good.

❖

Joy: age seven

"Why didn't she just be my mother? Why did she have me be adopted?" The questions tumbled out right after breakfast one morning. Luckily Teresa had the morning off, and she willed her racing heart to slow down, wanting to handle these questions in a calm way.

"Well, Daddy and I were told a few things about the woman who gave birth to you, dear, but not everything. We were told that she felt she couldn't take care of you, that she was too young to be a mother at that time. It had nothing to do with *you*, you know. You were a wonderful baby. What do you think it meant that she felt she was too young?"

"Maybe she didn't know how to change diapers?" seven-year-old Joy ventured.

"Well, maybe. Of course, she probably could have learned that. But I wonder what else?"

"I don't know."

"Do you think maybe she wanted to finish high school?"

"You mean she still went to school?"

"Yes, and she might have thought it would be hard for her to get a good job if she quit school then to take care of a baby. Or if she tried to do both, she might not do a good job being a mother."

"So she was a kid." The truth seemed to filter in slowly. Teresa waited, drinking coffee casually but fully available to Joy—for as long as the questions might take. "So she was a kid and she wanted to grow up."

"She was in high school, though," Teresa clarified. "She wasn't a little kid like you, but she probably still felt like she was too much of a kid to be a mom."

"Could she drive a car?"

"I don't know that, but I imagine she can by now."

The mundane and the insightful were intermingled in Joy's questions as she tried to understand her birthmother and her motivations. That was all for that day, Teresa realized as Joy drifted off into other activities, reading the back of the cereal box and slipping crusts from cinnamon toast to the dog.

More questions and emotions would undoubtedly follow. Perhaps piece by piece, perhaps in large gushes. Teresa would answer what she could and help Joy speculate on the rest, knowing that even speculation is beneficial since it narrows the possibilities. "It always seems to help when we talk about possibilities, even if they are only fantasy. That way I really know what Joy is thinking, and I can guide her if she seems too far off. It's better than my guessing what she's guessing!" Teresa explained to a friend later.

And then who could tell what the future would hold. Perhaps Joy would be one of the presently small but growing number of persons, currently 2 - 4% in the United States, who had been adopted and who decide as adults to meet the woman who gave birth to them. Perhaps she would not be among those.

Teresa felt comfortable with the conversation. She was neither discouraging nor encouraging her daughter along these lines. She felt she must be open but neutral and that Joy as an adult could and should and would make the best decision for herself when that time came.

❖

David: age eight

"Mom, where did I come from?" David asked his mother Lani one day when he was eight.

"What do you mean?" Lani asked.

"Well, what country were my birthmother and birthfather from? From America or from somewhere else?"

"Oh, Daddy and I have that information," Lani answered. "They were both born in America, but their families were Irish and Italian. You're part Irish and part Italian."

David's eyes lit up mischievously. "Well," he rejoined, "my face is Irish, but my tastebuds sure are Italian!"

❖

Jonathan: age eight

"When will I not be adopted anymore?" Jonathan asked from the back seat. "I'm really tired of being adopted."

Elizabeth and Joe had taken a route through Canada on the way to Grandma and Grandpa's house in Michigan. The subject arose when they encountered "Adopt A Road" signs in Canada identical to those they'd seen in every state through which they'd traveled. Elizabeth didn't exactly like the ubiquitous signs, feeling they trivialized adoption, but Joe felt they were at least positive and wasn't concerned about them. So the conversation went.

Until Jonathan's query: "When will I not be adopted anymore?"

It was a definite signal from their son: Isn't there something else to talk about? Do we have to have a long discussion about adoption whenever anything remotely reminds us of the topic?

"Perhaps," Elizabeth and Joe decided when they were alone later that evening, "we'd better keep this in perspective. Perhaps we're pushing it. There's probably a fine line between open-ness and over-dosing a child on the subject of adoption. Let's talk it over with Sally and Jim when we get home."

"Some people," Sally said when their families were together the follow-ing weekend, "seem to feel the *more* they can talk about adoption in the presence of or to their children—the better. Jim and I don't. We don't even tell Karl and Evan when we go to a post-adoptive services meeting, although we know one mother who told her children after a meeting that she had discussed with other parents the problems adopted children have! Honest! Talk about asking for trouble.

"As far as meetings go, we *do* tell our children when we're going to a fund-raiser for our agency. We tell them we're going to help raise money to help pay costs so that more people can adopt children. Now that's not an easy concept, either, but we think it's one that helps our children see how positively we feel about adoption—that we'll put time and en-ergy and money into helping other people adopt."

Jim added, "Who knows if this is right. It just seems to us that talking about adoption, like anything else, can be overdone to the point where the conversations are counterproductive, and I think that's what Jonathan was telling you by his comment. We feel the subject is certainly not to be avoided but also not one to be pounced upon at every opportunity. It's one facet of life and should be treated as such."

❖

Ashley: age eight

Ashley had always talked openly about adoption with her mother Carin. On several occasions Carin had presented Ashley, who was eight, with age-appropriate books on the subject.

Perhaps it was the timing, but this particular book was not received well by Ashley at that moment. It was one having to do with adoption and the feelings children might have about it, one that Carin knew many other children had loved reading.

"I don't need that book," Ashley said, pushing it back across the table toward her mother. "*You* need to read that book."

❖

Christiana: age eight

Leigh had been waiting for eight-year-old Christina to ask questions about her birthmother. The general questions about adoption had been asked and answered, but Christina had not asked for the particulars about her birthmother and why she had chosen adoption.

As Leigh was fixing dinner, she could hear Christina and her nine-year-old friend Kara "playing Barbies" again in the family room. The games were becoming more and more elaborate. The sofa cushions formed homes for the several dolls, who visitied each other and shared concerns. Leigh was glad Christina still liked to play with dolls. It seemed like healthy practice in relationships to her.

Suddenly Leigh caught her breath and listened, motionless. Christina's Barbie was drinking a soda and saying, "But if I had a baby and there wasn't a dad, then the baby and I could live with my mom and we could take care of the baby and everything."

"But maybe your mom wouldn't want to. Or maybe she wouldn't have room in her house," Kara's Barbie countered. With a slightly different tone, Kara went on. "My mom says we were lucky because Nana and Grandpa had a big house. I don't think it's a good idea."

Kara and her mother's heartbreaking story flashed through Leigh's mind as she stood listening. Newborn Kara and her mother had been abandoned by Kara's father when mother and daughter were both still in the hospital. He just never came to see them. The divorce papers arrived months later. Kara's mother had remarried just about a year ago, but they had lived with Kara's grandparents until then, nearly eight years. It had worked quite well, but evidently little Kara could sense a strain.

"Well, maybe the baby and I could live in a little house right next to my mom. Or maybe somebody would adopt the baby," Christina's Barbie said after a pause.

"Okay. Well, should we go to a movie? We have to change. Let's wear the new outfits," Kara's Barbie said as she rustled about.

Tears sprang to Leigh's eyes as she thought of the realities Christina and Kara had faced during those moments and during their short lives. How fortunate that they had each other at this time and that they had loving families. But Leigh's tears were replaced with a gentle smile. What mature thinking on the part of such little children. What awareness of the feelings of other people and of the difficult situations some people face. When it came time for Christina to talk about her birthmother, Leigh was sure Christina would understand.

❖

Katrina: age eight

Kate and her daughter Katrina were sitting in the car, contemplating getting out and hauling all the packages into the house. They'd had a pleasant day together, shopping, having lunch, shopping some more.

26

Katrina had been quiet for a while, and Kate knew something was on her mind. Suddenly she turned and said, "I'm a princess."

"You certainly are—my little princess," Kate began.

"No, no!" Katrina said adamantly. "I mean my mother was a queen."

Kate didn't do a good job of repressing the smile, knowing what a typical fantasy this is for a child who was adopted, or even for one who was not. Katrina caught the grin and reacted. "You'll never know how it feels to be adopted," she fairly yelled.

Kate didn't think quickly enough to say, "Can you tell me how it feels?" But she did accept her daughter's feelings, and she felt good that Katrina had been comfortable telling her mother, even insisting that she hear, what was on her mind.

❖

Prentiss: age nine

"Mom, will you tell me the story of when you first saw me at the adoption agency again? Here, I'll get a Kleenex, 'cause I know you're going to cry."

❖

Andrew: age nine

"If you didn't adopt me, then I'd be with my birthmother," Andrew said in an accusatory tone. "I wish I wasn't adopted."

It had been another hard day. The whole week had been hard. Andrew was becoming more and more resistant to the fact that his family was going to have to move in just over a month. At first he'd been excited about the adventure, but the fact that he would be leaving his friends was beginning to bother him. Missing his friends ... missing his birthmother. Karen guessed the thoughts were connected.

She tried the commiserative approach. "It sounds like you're missing your birthmother. Some kids, when they are going to move, realize they'll miss their friends, and it makes them miss other people, like birthmothers, too."

"Oh, Mom, you're always saying stuff like that to me. I just wish I wasn't adopted. I wish you hadn't taken me."

"Andrew, you weren't adopted just because we wanted you. Your birthmother decided on adoption because she didn't think she could take care of you then. You were a wonderful baby, but she just couldn't be a parent then. We met with her twice. She wanted you to be a part of our family. But, Andrew, if it hadn't been our family, there would have been another family to raise you."

Andrew didn't have more to say that day. Karen was concerned that she'd been too blunt, and perhaps a bit defensive, and yet there was a reality for Andrew to know. If he was harboring anger at his family for causing his adoption, he needed to understand. But what a hard time to say it—when the move was looming.

And then another thought occurred to Karen. Was there possible concern on Andrew's part that he might in reality be leaving his birthmother behind, that she might still be living somewhere in the area, something that Karen and her husband didn't know. Might Andrew be concerned that the move would actually distance him geographically from his birthmother?

Karen thought, "We'll need to come back to this later. Maybe we can talk about it more. Or maybe it's all right. Sometimes it's so hard to know ...."

❖

Joanna: age nine

The mothers were sipping tea, giving their daughters a few more minutes to play. "I think we have friends in common," Mary Alice said to Gail.

"Oh, how do you know the Greens?" Gail asked.

"Well, Joanna was telling us which adoption agency she came from, and we once lived next door to the Greens, who adopted from the same agency when we were neighbors."

As Gail and Joanna drove home, Gail said, "Honey, I understand you've been talking about our adoption agency."

"Well," she answered, "they asked me about my life, and I thought I'd start at the beginning."

❖

Jeremy: age twelve

"Do your kids ask how much you paid for them?" Lynda asked.

"Sure," Jan answered. "Once they even ganged up on me and wanted to know whom we paid the most for!"

"Well," Lynda continued, "I've told them all the information about the expenses of the agency, their caseworkers, legal consultants, birthmother expenses, et cetera, but now Jeremy is back asking again. 'Okay,' he says, 'if you didn't pay for me, then what were the agency's fees?' I don't know whether to tell him or not. Won't a time come when he's old enough to know this?"

"It's probably media interest that has triggered his interest," Jan said. "Articles and talk shows about baby-selling, with outrageous price tags attached.

"Whatever we decide to do when the children are older, I guess we must keep repeating *You don't pay for a child*. Because I think they're really asking, 'Did you pay for me?' And so we must keep saying 'No, *you don't buy a child*. You pay for services so that you can adopt a child.'"

"The children's questions may be prompted by their friends," Lynda suddenly interjected. "I just remembered a friend telling me that their son, whom they adopted from Colombia, is asked quite often by friends and even acquaintances in his middle school, 'How much did your parents pay for you?' This questioning has only been prevalent during the past few years, since their older daughter, also from Colombia, was never asked. It makes me think media treatment of adoption has given society, including children, the feeling that they can make these inappropriate queries.

"We have to encourage our children to answer this question as we answer them. 'You don't buy a child. You pay for services so that you can adopt a child.' If a friend persists, our children might counter, 'Well, how much did your parents pay for you? Being born costs something, too.' This might help their friends understand the expense of services involved."

❖

Lisa: age thirteen

"What made me think of it was when we were talking about green cards at school," Lisa explained. "Christy's mother was born in Austria, and so we were talking about which country Christy would be a citizen of, the United States or Austria. That just made me wonder where my birthparents were from before they came to this country."

Lisa had just asked her mother if she could find out more about her birthmother, and her birthfather, too, which happened to be the first time Lisa had asked about him. After talking over the options, they agreed that her mother would call the adoption agency to see if any more information were available besides what Lisa already had.

"I'd like them to send it to me if there is anything else. But if there isn't, that's okay, too. I'm just curious."

❖

31

Telling The Story

Suzannah: age fourteen

Julie knew she couldn't generalize from one experience, but it did serve to remind her once again that, in most cases, it's best to wait until a child asks before talking about adoption. This particular topic was an important one, and she was so glad she had waited. Her daughter Suzannah, fourteen, had finally brought it up herself, and now the uncomfortable feeling Julie had been harboring was gone.

It all revolved around the fact that Suzannah was—ah—in love. This was the first real boyfriend experience; the telephone was in constant use from the moment homework was completed until the cut-off hour, 9 p.m. Suzannah fairly glowed. She was allowed to go to movies or school functions with a group of friends, boys and girls. The limits were being obeyed. All was well.

Except that Julie had this nagging burden, was the word for it, that she should be doing something. She was aware from her reading that adolescence is often a time when young people who were adopted examine the fact once again and that the usual turmoil of these years can be heightened by any confusion or anger they might feel regarding their adoption. But most frightening was Julie's recollection of the precautions of a speaker at a meeting she and her husband had attended years earlier: that girls who are adopted might have a tendency to emulate the actions of their birthmothers and become sexually active at an early age, possibly becoming pregnant for any number of complex reasons.

Julie had never seen statistics on this assertion, and in her own experience, as she thought about friends' children, it wasn't the case. But it nagged at her. She had even asked another speaker at another meeting some years later if there were such statistics, and he had replied, "No. If a young woman who was herself adopted becomes pregnant at an early age and before marriage, something else is usually going on in the family, as is the case with any teenage girl."

That was comforting, but even he didn't have statistics. And what if the first speaker were correct? Should Julie talk to her daughter about her fears?

Another bit of advice Julie had been given over the years was that while it's generally best to wait for questions from your child, it won't hurt to bring up a subject you think may be on his mind, especially if you've gotten some hints that there are unasked questions waiting to emerge. Third-person comments are often helpful: "Some kids at your age start thinking about their birthmothers...."

And that was fine on a birthday or Mother's Day. But sex and having babies? Should Julie bring this up?

"No, good grief, no!" the friend she called nearly shouted into the phone. "Julie, this *is* a time to talk with Suzannah about sex. Wouldn't you have this talk with her whether she was adopted or born into your family? But bringing up her birthmother in a discussion about sex isn't germane at this point. No, no, no!"

The burden lifted, and Julie knew she'd been caught in the trap of having listened too seriously to one-too-many experts. She knew she needed to listen and read and then follow her own hunches, which had always proven correct. Perhaps it was the high valence of this subject that made Julie mistrust her own judgment.

And that night at bedtime, Suzannah had brought up her birthmother and some questions that had just occurred to her. Yes, adoption and birthmother had been on Suzannah's mind, but not in the context that had concerned Julie.

Julie shuddered. Yes, she would soon talk again and in depth about sex and responsibility and urges of the teen years. But if she had brought up birthmother and pregnancy at this precious point in time, when Suzannah was truly beginning to think of herself as a young woman and was thinking so positively about herself and her first real relationship with a young man, Julie felt she might have confused the issues.

"Adoptive parents must not hide their heads in the sand," Julie thought, "but neither must they look for trouble. I wonder if there isn't a real possibility of setting in motion a self-fulfilling prophesy. Without being naive, I think a little more optimism might be in order."

❖

Regina: age fifteen

"My daughter's country of birth is a very poor one," Andrea explained, "and though we've tried to emphasize the positive, floods and other natural disasters that take place there are constantly making headlines."

Regina, a very intelligent fifteen-year-old, was usually quite reserved, and so it took Andrea a bit by surprise when her daughter, after reading an especially sad account of the latest flood, said, "How could I have been so lucky? I know I could easily have died if I'd remained there as a baby. I ache for those people. I even feel a little guilty."

And then the more personal concern surfaced. "Do you think my birthmother had other children?"

"I wonder that sometimes myself, dear," Andrea said gently. "Your dad and I found out everything we could when we were there, but there wasn't much to be learned, and you know it all. We've never heard more, although we told the agency we would like to be updated on any information they receive. The silence could mean so many different things."

"If there were any other children, I wish they could be here with us." Tears formed in Regina's eyes.

"So do I," Andrea said. "Of course, maybe there were no more children. Or maybe there were and they are fine. I wonder if it might be time for you to write the agency and ask if there is more information. Regina, I doubt that there will be, but at least you'll have tried everything you can."

"Mom, I'm so lucky. I'm so lucky."

"Sweetheart, we're all lucky. We're lucky to be a family."

❖

Indre, Joseph, Leah: teen to teen

"I'm trying to find a situation where I can live with a family for a few weeks so that I can experience the culture," Indre said. "I don't want to just be a tourist there."

"I do," Joseph interrupted. "I just want to see everything I've read about all these years. My grandparents have been keeping a scrapbook for me, and I want to see it all first hand."

"I want to do that, but I also want to check with my agency, if it's still there, to see if I can get any health records. I mainly want to go there to find out more about me, I guess," Leah said.

The high school students, all adopted internationally, were meeting once a month. Their collective dream was a graduation trip to the lands of their birth. Some wanted to travel with their parents. Some wanted to make this journey with a friend. Some hoped to travel soon. Some hoped it could be later.

Some would probably accomplish the dream. Others knew, despite their group money-making efforts, that for the time being, it was only a dream. But even they valued the meetings where they could talk about their interests and wishes. It was nice to gather with others who had two important traits in common: their families were not the ones they'd been born into, and their country was not the one of their birth.

The students had started meeting all on their own. Each person seemed to know one or two other persons who would like to join, and soon they were nine.

"I wish we'd done this when we were kids," Indre said.

"Oh, but then it would have been our parents deal, and now it's ours."

❖

Adult to adult

"Why is it always 'Mom, Mom' when a tricky question is on its way?" Bonnie laughingly asked her husband Paul. "Why isn't it 'Dad, Dad' once in a while?"

Bonnie was relating the latest of their daughter's questions about her adoption, the ones that all tumbled out the year Stephanie was seven. She had scarcely caught her breath from one question before another would issue forth. Bonnie had read a lot. She'd thought a lot. She'd talked with numerous friends who were adoptive parents. Her mind seemed to go into high gear when the questions came, she was thankful to say, and she was usually pleased with the outcome of the exchange.

"And Paul is always there to listen afterwards, to support me and encourage me. But in all fairness ..." Bonnie laughed.

"I'm only kidding," she added. "I consider it a privilege that our daughter comes to me, so grateful that she talks to one of us. Some children do talk more regularly to their dads about adoption, by the way, but most often it's mom. Some children broach the subject reluctantly or seldom. I think we're very fortunate.

"I am, seriously, being facetious about the fairness of it all. The fact that I bring it up at all is telling, however. Each such exchange takes an enormous amount of emotional energy on my part. I'm thrilled to be able to offer it to our daughter, thrilled that we can communicate so readily about adoption and everything else. My only reason for bringing it up is to let parents know that they are not the only ones who may be exhausted by the exchanges."

❖

Adult to adult

"We know we're to tell the truth," Claire ventured, "but we also need to consider what might put an undue burden on our children. Is that what you understood the speaker last night to say?"

"Right," Joan agreed. "And it makes good sense. It would be easy to truthfully tell our kids how empty and unhappy we felt before they came to us."

"But that gives children the burden of thinking they're responsible for their parents' happiness. Best leave that part out," Claire added. "And we needn't view that as being secretive with our children. We as parents decide if and when to tell any number of things to our children about other subjects. This one is no different."

"Just assuring them of our love, of how glad we are we're a family, of how we're a family forever. That's the security they need—and that's what's important."

❖

Adult to adult

Susan had married when she was in her early thirties, and she was hoping to start a family as soon as possible. She was delighted, then, when pregnancy happened quickly and her son Christopher was born, healthy and beautiful.

Susan had herself been adopted as an infant, and since her friend Mandy had adopted a daughter, Susan and Mandy had had numerous conversations about the subject over the years. Susan had always been very positive about her adoption, perhaps, in retrospect, overly positive.

Susan had really never had probing conversations with her mother about the adoption even though she knew she and her sister had been adopted.

It had just never seemed important. She had loved her parents. What more was there to it.

It caught Mandy by surprise, then, when Susan phoned when her son was nearly two months old.

"It's just hit me," Susan confided, and Mandy knew she was crying. "I'm sitting here with Christopher in my lap. And all of a sudden I think, 'How could she do it? How could my birthmother possibly give me away?'" And then she added poignantly the same words Mandy's daughter had asked when she was seven. "Was I so terrible?"

"No, Susan, no!" Mandy answered as she had answered her daughter. "It wasn't you. You were perfect. I'm sure you were—look at you now! The problem was not you. The problem was she was probably too young to be a parent. I'm sure it was the hardest thing she's ever done in her life."

This opened a door for Susan. She had never wanted to ask questions, she realized, because she didn't want to seem disloyal to her parents whom she loved so much. That same feeling remained, and Susan felt it would be very hard on her parents, now near seventy, if she were to begin asking about her adoption at this point, and she wanted to follow her instincts.

There were other avenues open to her. Susan had been adopted in one of the few states which makes available upon request many of the adoption records. She mailed her self-addressed stamped envelope and waited.

The packet arrived, and Susan pored over it for days, first alone and then with her husband. She knew how to make a second request that would bring a name to her.

Now, a year and a half later, Susan hasn't taken that second step. She says she's not closing the door, that some day she may decide to find out more, perhaps even see if her birthmother would be in favor of being contacted. At present, though, Susan is at peace with the issue and feels comfortable "leaving things as they are."

The fact that Susan's concerns surfaced at all, which is not uncommon when an adopted person reaches a landmark in life such as marriage, birth of a child, the death of a parent, is instructive. "The catharsis seemed to be needed at some point in time," Mandy thought. "If Susan had had the information earlier, would the questions about her adoption have been easier to handle at this point? We'll never know. Will my daughter go through this if she bears a child? We'll only know when the time comes. If so, I hope she will be comforted by knowing she's not alone and I hope someone will be there for her."

Susan took a slightly different approach to these thoughts when Mandy shared them with her. "I'm actually glad, in retrospect, that everything happened for me in the time and way that it did. I can imagine the muddle I would have made of this as a teenager or even as a young adult. Now I'm older and settled and comfortable with my life, and for me, the timing was right, probably because of the perspective I have on life at my age, since I'm married and have a child of my own."

Susan made one additional observation about Mandy's approach to talking about adoption with her daughter. "This observation may, in fact, not be a very popular one," Mandy warned, "but it was an honest reaction of someone quite involved with the issue, someone who is a very thoughtful and intelligent person, and someone who deserves the right to her opinion."

Susan said one day, "You know, I'm not so sure but what I'm glad my parents were just a bit jealous of me, if that's the word. They must have in some way communicated to me, though not verbally, that they would have been threatened if I showed too much interest in my birthmother. It was somehow a very secure feeling.

"I listen to you and other adoptive mothers talk, and though I appreciate your wish to be open about the subject with your children, I almost feel you are overdoing it sometimes. Some of the mothers seem to bring it up every time an occasion arises. They seem to me to be ready to 'pounce' upon the topic whenever they can. I wonder if you don't need to be careful that your children don't feel obligated to eventually try to locate their birthparents. I wonder if they won't feel something is wrong with them if they decide not to. I wonder if they don't feel a bit pushed away by you."

Susan continued, "I realize this feeling may be a rationalization for my present decision. But this thought won't leave me, and I think it's worth some analysis on your part."

"I am grateful that Susan shared her insights with me," Mandy decided. "I've taken her precautionary words seriously, and I hope I can achieve a balance in my quest to help my daughter feel comfortable with her own situation. I hope she can feel that my love for her and my confidence in our relationship frees her to follow the course she thinks is best, but I also hope my openness is not interpreted as pressure. The amount of information each adopted individual requires about his past is strictly personal. I hope my daughter will realize that above all, and that she will avoid pressures or 'guilt trips' imposed by me or anyone else as she chooses what is right for her."

❖

Chapter Three
Do I Really Belong?

Every preschool child, born or adopted into his family, needs a repetition of facts. He can't be told anything "once and for all." He needs to hear it again and again.

"No matter what, you're ours forever and ever," his mother assured him.

"Forever and ever, amen," Daniel said with satisfaction and a sigh.

Preschoolers' concerns reported by parents who were interviewed for **Dialogues** seemed to have one focus: "Am I your forever child?" Even if the question sometimes came out backward or with anger, wise parents could read their child's actual concern. Over and over, parents of preschoolers assured their children whom they had adopted: "Forever and ever."

A teacher's understanding of the seven-year-old child is instructive as we consider the adopted school-aged child's possible concerns about belonging. The teacher of seven-year-olds realizes that students, adopted or born into their families, often feel at this age that "nobody likes me." The seven-year-old likes to touch base frequently with the teacher, showing a need for security, but also showing normal, healthy movement away from focus on family to focus on school. The teacher of seven-year-olds responds by creating structure within the classroom, which

43

promotes a feeling of security on the part of the students, and by giving them constant reinforcement.

Might the child who was adopted into his family, and who might on occasion wonder if he really belongs, display these seven-year-old tendencies, and need the same structure and reinforcement?

Adolescence, often that time of the "first love," can create conflict within the adolescent. As he "falls in love" with members of the opposite sex, he may feel he is withdrawing love from his family, which makes him feel quilty. His solution? Perhaps fight with parents, find fault with them, and therefore feel less guilty about withdrawing love. Conflicts between parents and adolescents can actually be "trumped up" in order to alleviate the adolescent's guilt.

Might the adolescent who was adopted experience the same or even intensified guilt, feel disloyal to adoptive parents, and perhaps even use adoption as a subject of conflict?

The adolescent, adopted or born into his family, who is experiencing such conflict, usually doesn't want his parents' physical affection at that time as much as he wants a sympathetic attitude toward his problems and a tolerance of his mood swings. While perhaps the language is more sophisticated, even the critical adolescent can still be asking the same question: "Do I really belong?" And the answer, as can be inferred from the following vignettes, is still the same. "You're ours, forever and ever."

❖

Do I Really Belong?

Lauren: age two

"It was one of those times when I picked up the right book at the right time," Sarah began. "Day after day, my daughter, Lauren, whom we had just adopted at age two, would sit on my lap, would cooperate in every respect, but she wouldn't look at me.

"She finally began looking at my son and then at my husband, Richard. In fact, I think my son was responsible for the breakthrough. Lauren was fascinated by Bryan. She had been with a loving foster family for five months, and she had become very attached to them. They had no other young children in the house, however, and so Lauren now seemed drawn to Bryan.

"A whole month had gone by, and Lauren had still never made voluntary eye contact with me. And then I picked up one of Dr. Brazelton's books which seemed to fall open to the chapter telling how a child adopted at over two years of age will often experience four to six weeks of grieving.

"I breathed a sigh of relief to know this was an expected process. I instantly realized that Lauren's reluctance to look at me was her way of holding on to the wonderful foster mother who had raised her for several months and to whom she was deeply attached. She really didn't want to let me in—not yet. It hadn't been as hard for her to relate to Richard. He was a man. He wasn't replacing her foster mother.

"And so I knew it would take time, and that gradually, gradually, Lauren could find a place for me in her heart.

"This knowledge was a relief, true, but it came with its own price. I'm afraid I then began to feel guilty because we had 'dislodged' Lauren from such a loving foster family where she felt so comfortable. And somewhere in the recesses of my heart I was even feeling guilty about Lauren's birthmother, whom I'd never met. 'I get to raise this precious little girl,' I thought. 'I feel so sad for her birthmother.' My guilt was irrational. The foster family was not able to adopt Lauren, and her birthmother was not able to raise her.

"The resolution came gradually. I came to grips with my own feelings after talking with many friends and with our caseworker. Lauren slowly began to relax more and more in my arms, and finally one day she spontaneously hugged me when we were laughing together at something.

"Lauren seemed to take one emotional step at a time. When she began to accept me, she pushed my husband away for a time. This, too, gradually disappeared as Richard stayed available for Lauren but understood her need to focus on me for a while.

"Lauren is now a bouncy, happy five-year-old. I would call our bond very strong. We've been through a lot together, and I feel this history has given each member of our family a profound respect and depth of feeling for each other."

❖

Marianna: age three

"Our agency had carefully explained the grieving process that our toddler would undoubtedly go through," Madeline said. "We were, after all, removing her from everything that was familiar in Colombia. She'd been in a foster home for many months. She might feel the separation from that family as well. It was hard to say when the grieving would become evident. She might have difficulty in bonding very quickly.

"It all happened, and I was so grateful for the preparation. It's just that it didn't happen in any order we expected, a reminder to us all, of course, that we must see each child as an individual.

"First of all, Marianna fairly flew into my arms at our first meeting, and I still feel the bonding was instantaneous. She was old enough to understand, after all, that she would now forever be a part of our family, that there would be no more changes for her.

"All the while we were in Colombia, she stayed as close to me as was physically possible. There was no doubt—Marianna was my little girl. She would go to my husband when asked and certainly seemed comfortable with him, but she clung to me.

"Marianna showed no outward concern about leaving the country of her birth. Nor did she seem to have any difficulty meeting her new sister or becoming accustomed to her new home. She simply showed excitement or interest about everything. Each day was an adventure!

"Of course it hit eventually. It was six months later. Somehow we weren't expecting it then, probably because everything had gone so incredibly smoothly.

"Now Marianna began having trouble sleeping, especially going to sleep. I would lie by her while she sobbed and sobbed, and I finally realized: This is the grieving process. In three-year-old language, partly Spanish and partly English, Marianna told me how she missed her birthmother, although later I wondered whether she was missing someone from her foster family as well.

"I encouraged her to talk, as I'd been coached to do. One answer surprised me. I had asked her, 'Honey, what can you tell me about your first mother? Do you remember her?'

"No," she replied. She couldn't remember her, but she missed her.

"I kept assuring Marianna that I knew it must feel bad, that I understood how she must miss her.

"I was amazed to realize one other thing. Even at three years of age, Marianna seemed to feel guilty talking to me about her sadness. She loved me, and I'm assuming that this was a three-year-old's feeling of disloyalty to me, with perhaps some fear of what disloyalty might bring.

"Of course I did my best to assure her that it was okay, that I knew she could love me and still miss her birthmother. We talked and talked, in English and Spanish. I had no trouble understanding her feelings even if I missed some of the words.

"Marianna's big sister, Caroline, who is instinctively motherly, probably helped her through this period more than anyone else. She knew Marianna needed cuddling and loving and gentle playing, and she provided her amply with these.

"I look back on it now and realize, over two years later, that even that difficult period, for Marianna and for all of us, was eased by the education my husband and I had received. We talked over and over again about how thankful we were for the preparation our agency had given us. If I hadn't known it was coming, I once said, I think I might have 'freaked!' It was scary, I guess is the word, to realize that Marianna's emotional well-being depended to a large part on how our family responded to her grieving and helped her through it. Knowing that is was a natural and expected phase was what helped us all handle it and made it possible for us, in turn, to help Marianna.

"I haven't mentioned my husband much during this story, and that's because there wasn't much direct interaction between him and Marianna up through this time. She had become quickly attached to me, as I have said, and next to her sister. There had been males in her life in Colombia, and so it wasn't a matter of her not knowing how to relate to men. We were puzzled. Finally we called our caseworker to see if there was an explanation or an approach we had overlooked."

"It's perfectly usual," the caseworker explained. "Marianna can only attach to one person at a time. It will just take a little longer. Since fathers usually aren't as available, the attachment is often to mothers first."

"Again, it worked," Madeline continued. "Summer was coming, and we decided on a quiet vacation on the rocky coastline of Maine. There were chipmunks to feed and waves to chase and picnics to pack and trails to follow. We were all perfectly relaxed, and of course Don was with the girls every minute. In fact, sometimes I would purposely read a book in the hammock, giving the girls time alone with him.

"That was what it took. We could almost see the attachment happening, and it filled us with joy. Besides making our family feel 'complete,' we knew this was another hurdle that Marianna had crossed as she learned to feel that she was definitely part of her new family."

❖

Do I Really Belong?

Daniel: age five

"Mommy, when you and Daddy got me, when I was a little baby, did you know that I would be bad?"

Margot replied, "Oh, yes, we knew you'd be *very* bad, like all kids, sometimes ... and no matter what, you're ours forever and ever."

"Forever and ever, amen," said Daniel with satisfaction and a sigh.

❖

Lauren: age five

Joanna had driven her daughter up to the synagogue, but Lauren wasn't ready to get out of the car.

"It's about this being Jewish," the rather articulate five-year-old Lauren began. "Jewish. I don't know."

"Lauren, our family is Jewish. You're Jewish," Joanna responded.

"But what about my birthmother. Maybe she wasn't Jewish."

"But you're part of our family, dear. When you're older, you can choose these things for yourself. Right now—it's off to the synagogue."

Joanna made a mental note to revisit the subject of the family religion later with Lauren. Perhaps there was some underlying issue that needed discussing. At that moment, however, setting limits had seemed to Joanna to be more important.

Do I Really Belong?

Todd: age six

Todd was angry at his mother and searching around for something that would really hit home, and so he came up with, "You weren't my first mother anyway."

"So what? I'm your mother now and I'm the mother of this house," Jeanne replied quickly and easily, thanks to the preparation she had gotten from her parent support group.

❖

Julie: age six

Julie, whom the Carsons had adopted from Korea as an infant, and her mother Ginny were walking home from school. Holding her mother's hand tightly, Ginny looked up and said, "Mommy, I wish I looked like you."

"It would be easier, wouldn't it?" Ginny responded. "But, Julie, if you looked like me, you wouldn't be you. And if I looked like you, I wouldn't be me. I'd be some other lady. And I'm glad I'm me and that you're my little girl."

Julie walked along thoughtfully for a moment and then responded. At first Ginny thought Julie hadn't understood, but perhaps she had. "I know if there had been a baby in your tummy, it would have been me."

❖

Do I Really Belong?

Sara: age six

After a particularly trying morning, six-year-old Sara announced, bags packed, that she was running away.

"No, you may not run away," Maureen said firmly.

"But you don't love me and I'm running away."

"You may not run away. I will always find you and bring you back where you belong," her mother said. "Remember *The Run-Away Bunny*? The bunny's mother would always find him and bring him back. And I do love you even if we have had a hard morning."

"I'm still running away," Sara insisted.

"You may go out in the front yard but you may not go out of the gate. And when you're ready, we have cookies and milk here."

"All right. I guess I'll be back...."

"The above scenario was the last in a series," Maureen reported. "Twice prior to this Sara had made similar declarations about running away. I had read somewhere that a parent shouldn't worry about such threats and should treat them lightly with a 'Don't forget your jacket; it's chilly outside.'

"Sara never actually ran away, but I was concerned that the thought kept recurring to her, and so I called a child psychiatrist who had dealt with many adopted children over the years.

"It was suggested that I purchase *The Run-Away Bunny* and read it casually to Sara at a time when she was not in a run-away mood,"

Maureen said. "I was told that any child, but especially an adopted child, will often test to see if she really does belong, if she really is loved. There always was to be absolute surety in my voice when I responded to her, firmness which assured Sara I was in charge, insistance that this was where she belonged."

Once these words were said, Sara never again talked of running away.

❖

Lia: age seven

"Mom, Mom," second-grader Lia announced as she jumped into the car after school. "Baby spiders don't stay with their moms long after they are born."

"Hmmm," Marcia responded, knowing how children often identify with little animals, and that separation concerns, while important for all children, might be deeper for the child who was adopted. "I wonder how the baby spiders feel about that."

"Well, I guess they grow up very fast and are ready to leave their mothers. I won't, though. I want to stay with you forever."

"And you may, honey," Marcia assured her. "Funny thing, though. When girls get old enough, they usually want to be on their own, just like those spiders. Someday you'll probably want to be on your own and do things without me. But that will be a long time from now, and by that time, you'll be all ready for it."

Lia looked slightly less than convinced, and so Marcia continued. "Remember when you were sure you didn't want to leave first grade? That you'd never be ready for second? And then, by the time second grade actually came, you were ready for it and love it."

That seemed to be the assurance she needed. "Today," Lia boasted, "we subtracted numbers with three digits, and I could do it!"

❖

Meg: age eight

After realizing that her 18-year-old friend, Britt, had left home and was living on a college campus, Monica's daughter Meg, who had been adopted as an infant, said wistfully, "Mom, will I have to go to college when I'm 18?"

"Oh, you don't have to," Monica replied. "But you may want to."

"No, I never want to leave you and Daddy. Can I live with you forever?"

"Certainly you can if that's what you choose, dear," Monica assured her. "Often when kids get that old, they want to live away from their parents. But we'll wait and see. Maybe you will and maybe you won't."

"You mean Britt wanted to leave home to go to college?"

"Oh, yes. She was a tiny bit scared, but she really wanted to. And she's enjoying it a lot."

"Oh."

Do I Really Belong?

Blair: age eight

Blair was eight and had been very verbal about his adoption during the past several years. This day he surprised Lucy with the assertion, "Mom, I'm glad I didn't grow in your tummy."

"You are?" Lucy replied. "That's interesting, because I kind of wish you had."

"Oh, but Mom," he said with a twinkle in his eye, "you like such spicy food, and if I had grown in your tummy, I'd have eaten that, and ...yuk!"

It's a precious statement to Lucy. "It's no doubt a rationalization on Blair's part, to be sure," she says, "but it tells me he's quite comfortable with his adoption—and he wanted me to know it."

❖

Tessa: age ten

Michelle's ten-year-old daughter Tessa was involved in a Shakespearean Festival at school on the occasion of that writer's 200th birthday, and her classmates had been asked to copy one of his "love sonnets," as they were referred to by the giggling girls in the class.

"I'm going to send my love sonnet to my cousin Billy," Tessa informed Michelle. "Sarah says I can marry Billy because we're not blood relatives."

"Billy is a neat kid, isn't he?" Michelle responded. "But, honey, he is your cousin, and cousins can't marry each other."

"But we're not blood relatives. I'm adopted."

Michelle sensed something beyond the superficial question, something which cried out "please assure me that I belong." And so she gently continued.

"You are definitely cousins, honey. It doesn't matter if you're born into a family or adopted into a family. You are a part of the family."

Silence.

And then, "Oh, okay. Oh, Mom, could we make me a flowered headband? They wore those during Elizabethan times, you know."

❖

Christy: age ten

"I'm not sure what to tell my daughter, because I have this nagging sense that she's right," Connie said. "Christy has said more that once that she thinks Grandma and Grandpa prefer her cousins, my brother's children, because they were born into the family. 'They don't love me as much because I was adopted,' she'll say.

"I try to help Christy look at other possibilities without denying her feelings. I have said, 'Maybe Grandma and Grandpa feel they know Aaron and Lexie better.' The truth is, I always felt my parents doted on my brother just a bit more than on me, and so I have said to Christy, 'Maybe it's just that Grandma and Grandpa are more comfortable with Uncle Colin than they are with our family. They all seem to like doing the same things. Maybe it has more to do with other people than with you, Christy. Of course, you may be right, but I'd be very sad for Grandma and Grandpa if they feel that way.'"

"What could possibly be sustaining their feelings, if indeed Christy is right?" Connie's friend Margaret, also an adoptive mother, asked. "Can it be that they're still wishing for the the bloodline after all these years? Christy couldn't be a neater kid. You'd think her way of entering the family would fade in their minds and they'd just look at all three children as their grandchildren."

"I've thought every once in a while of the grieving process Bruce and I went through after we learned I'd probably never conceive," Connie answered. "When we decided to adopt a child, our agency helped us even more to understand our feelings of loss—the loss of that child we'd never bear. We've maintained a good relationship with our caseworker, and even now, every once in a while, we'll call her about some questions Christy has. Bruce and I will inevitably end up gaining something for ourselves as well as for Christy, some deeper understanding of the adoption process and what it might mean to Christy at each stage of her life—as well as what it might mean for us as parents.

"And it occurs to me ... grandparents rarely if ever receive help through this process. And there is a loss for them, too. Not just bloodline, but they certainly must feel a sadness about their own child's sadness.

"Perhaps new adoptive parents need to be encouraged to talk about their own grieving process with their parents—unless that's asking too much of them at that time in their lives. Or maybe agencies and parent support groups could arrange Grandparents' Night."

"Maybe we're being too hard on them," Margaret offered. "You're making it sound like grandparents as a group do pretty well, considering how little formal support is available to them."

"Well, when you think of all the adoptive parents that talk about how pleased and proud they are of their extended families, I'd say they do very well as a group. But perhaps some conversations about the subject would he helpful to everyone, and probably could be extremely helpful to those with real difficulty."

❖

Hillary: age eleven

Hillary was eleven at the time, had asked every question in the book about her adoption, and had talked about it extensively with many of her friends.

One day, while playing at her best friend Debbie's house, Hillary mentioned to Debbie and her mother, "Well, my mom's tall and my dad's tall, so I'll be tall."

Debbie's mother Sue let the statement and the moment pass, and later in private related the incident to Hillary's mother Joy, wondering if she should have corrected Hillary's misconception.

How glad Joy was that she hadn't. How glad she was that her daughter could identify with her family in such a carefree way. "Hillary understands the biology involved," Joy said. "We've had conversations about the height of the man and woman who gave birth to her. This instance, I believe, was a knowing flight of fancy, a harmless and beautiful way of saying, 'I belong'."

❖

Do I Really Belong?

Julie: age eleven

Adele's daughter was pre-adolescent, which is probably all the explanation necessary. Tension had been building between them for weeks with very little respite. Although Adele was aware of Julie's growing need for independence, there were some limits, and she knew she was not being unreasonable.

Finally Julie's frustration tumbled out, and rather loudly. She had a hard time obeying Adele, she said, because she didn't think of her as her real mother.

"Oh, yes, I am your real mother," Adele insisted. "I'll always be your mother. You're stuck with me!"

❖

Tim: age eleven

Steve was rather "all thumbs" when it came to anything mechanical, and so he was delighted to realize his son Tim, now eleven, whom the Wrights had adopted as an infant, was quite mechanically inclined.

Steve's spontaneous and beautiful remark when Tim first fixed something that his dad had been struggling with was, "Wow, you're a lot better at this than I am. You must get that ability from your side of the family!"

Steve had affirmed everyone in that statement. He showed that he valued Tim's ability, valued his biological background, and he confirmed Tim's place in the Wright family, a family that has several "sides" to it.

Do I Really Belong?

Jo: age twelve

"My daughter Jo's onset of puberty seemed to be the catalyst for adoption conversations again. She'd asked so many questions when she was seven, but since then the issue has seldom arisen," Patrice said.

"I've read that a number of the milestones in the life of a person who had been adopted could bring the issue to the forefront. Here was one of them for my daughter. Others included, according to the article I read, marriage, birth of the adopted person's own child, death of a parent or someone close.

"I could understand that each of these times was quite likely a time of introspection for every person, and for the person who had been adopted, introspection could likely include another examination of the adoption. I was glad to know this ahead of time and was expecially attuned to comments from my daughter that might be adoption related.

"In this case, as the hormones took over, my daughter's mood swings were incredible, as so often happens. Therefore it became increasingly difficult to converse about adoption or any subject.

"It was so obvious what was happening, however, that I didn't let it bother me. If something seemed adoption-related and important, I brought it up at the best moment I could find, even if I'd get an angry, 'No, that's stupid!' in reply. I knew she'd heard me, and I could sense her relief.

"Sometimes when girls reach puberty, they realize they can be mothers themselves some day, and it makes them think a lot more about their birthmothers," I ventured to Jo at one point.

"'No, that's not it!' was the reply, and I let it go at that," Patrice continued. "If in fact the thought had not been on her mind, I didn't want to insist or overemphasize it, which I felt could do more harm than good. If, on the other hand, the thought had occurred to her—and I sensed that it had—my bringing it out in the open could let her know that the subject was perfectly all right to discuss, that the thought was a rather common one for a person who had been adopted, and that no topic need be considered out of bounds between us.

"One unusual but poignant exchange let me know I was on the right track. 'Thanks for being so nice and not being mad at me, Mom,' my daughter whispered one night as I was tucking her in. 'I don't know why I get so grouchy. Sometimes I just feel crabby from the inside.'

"It's called hormones, honey," Patrice responded, amazed at her daughter's insight. "And I'll always love you, grouchies and all."

❖

Tom: young adult

Tom was laughing when his mother Char answered the phone. He was calling, he said, to see if she had any more of his medical records than he already knew about.

Char and Robert had learned all they could about Tom's birthparents' health records at the time of the adoption and had passed the records on to their son, but now that Tom was entering the hospital for minor surgery, he had specific questions. Had there ever been diabetes in his birthfamily? Heart disease? Strokes?

Tom said, "I'll explain why I was laughing. You'll never believe what I just did. The nurse gave me a form on which I was to record family health history, and I was writing yours and dad's. Then I remembered I was adopted!"

"Do you think there's any question about whether Tom feels he's part of our family?" Char asked her husband that evening as she related the story to him.

❖

Adult to adult

"I'm forever grateful to a speaker at a parents' meeting who prepared me for the day my child might use the zinger," Alice said. "It's a favorite way to resist, and it's one assertion that can really be felt by the adoptive parent who doesn't know it's coming: 'I don't have to go to bed. You're not my *real* mother.'

"It can come in several guises. 'My real mother wouldn't make me go to bed.' 'You don't own me. I wasn't born to you.'

"The answer to all of the above, calmly but firmly stated, must always be: 'Oh, yes, I *am* your real mother, and it's bedtime.'

"It's not difficult to read between the lines," the speaker had said, "to realize the child probably needs to be assured he does in fact belong, that his mother is in charge, that he is safe, even if he should add 'I hate you!' to any of his assertions."

"Our speaker had another creative one-liner for the persistent child. 'My *real* mother would be nicer' can be handled with an equally calm but firm, 'Be that as it may, it is time for bed.' "

Do I Really Belong?

Adult to adult

Sue finds the insensitivity of the questions and comments people, often perfect strangers, feel they can make regarding adopted children truly amazing. People have on occasion, on learning that she has adopted a child, proceeded to tell her the latest findings they have just read in one magazine or another—most of them with no convincing studies attached—that explain various problems exhibited by adopted children.

"It's their tone of voice and attitude that bother me," Sue explained. "They never tell me stuff like this about my children who were born to me, and heaven knows you can find discouraging studies about *any* child if you've a mind to. But their tone of voice is one which assumes a certain detachment on my part. I don't believe I'm reading anything into it. I really feel that *they* feel I'm not as attached, not as bonded, not as involved emotionally with my child that I adopted as compared with those born to me. And in this context, I haven't any idea of how to counter this ridiculous assumption. I counter the articles to which they are referring—but I don't know how to dissipate that attitude.

"Thank goodness," Sue added quickly, "this kind of thing is relatively rare. Most people recognize my child for what she is: my child. And I bring up this problem not so much because it makes *me* uncomfortable as for my concern that this attitude might be conveyed to my children or to other children. My children, born to me or adopted by me, must not feel that I am scrutinizing them for potential problems, expecting problems. If problems do arise, we'll deal with them, as we would the problems any child faces. But my children, adopted or born to me, simply need to feel unconditional love, unconditional belonging, my faith in them, and the joy of growing up. We parents can help by encouraging each other.

Do I Really Belong?

"How can I say it. As an adoptive parent, I ache for my child if she has a problem just as much as do those of you whose children were born to you. Please recognize this similarity and be *as* thoughtful of me, but not more so, as you are to your friends with biological children."

❖

Adult to adult

"It's probably my English teacher background, but I'm very aware of how I use the word 'adopted'," Gayle began.

"First of all, I make the verb tense as 'past' as possible. I never say, for example, that my son 'is' adopted. I say he 'was' adopted. The adoption was an action that took place nearly ten years ago. I'm not denying his adoption, but I see no need to make it sound like it's anything less than totally permanent.

"In addition, I'm careful where I place the word 'adopted' in a sentence where it's being used as an adjective. My son is not my 'adopted' son. He is my son whom we adopted, should I ever need to refer to him in that way. I don't want 'adopted' between my son and me.

"Picky? Possibly. But with such little effort, we parents can say to our children on yet another level 'You belong.' Difficult to remember? Not really. Once the mind-set is there, it doesn't take much practice until the old way of saying it just doesn't feel right anymore."

❖

64

Do I Really Belong?

Adult to adult

"Although this amounts to a stereotyping of adoptive parents, I think it's worth taking the chance of saying it. I'll speak for myself and my experience, and then other parents can accept or reject the thoughts as they apply to themselves," Karen said.

"My husband and I fit so many categories. First of all, we're older parents. I was 35 when our older child came to us, nearly 40 when our younger child was born to us. We'd waited so long. We were so thrilled. It was difficult for us to be disciplinarians. It was easy for us to 'understand' the dynamics of what was happening and not take action.

"We caught it in the nick of time by reading everything we could get our hands on. We finally realized that our children, adopted or biological, only feel safe if they know we are in charge. That, adopted or biological, they want limits even if they will test them. That, biological or adopted, we owe our children the training of which discipline is a part.

"That, adopted or biological, they are happier, as are we, if they are acting 'right.' That, biological or adopted, they need to be treated just the same. And then, adopted or biological, they will know that they really belong."

❖

66

Chapter Four
Looking Like Parents

In a day when physical matching of a child with his new adoptive family is considered unimportant, and is in fact frowned upon in some circles, "looking like parents" can still become an issue even for a child in a same-race adoption. It happens that only a few of the stories in this chapter were offered by such families, however. The preponderance were from those who adopted their children transracially. All stories are instructive to everyone.

The preschool child, unaccustomed to thinking abstractly, can repeat his adoption story but understands it only on a superficial level, which is appropriate at that stage. While the preschooler who was adopted transracially is at the same non-abstract level in his thinking, he has noticed the different skin tone or hair texture by this time and usually will ask about it.

While he may ask again and again when his hair will look like daddy's, for instance, it may be the intuitive feelings on the part of the preschooler, who seems to be able to sense even uncertainty, that make a more lasting impression than will the actual answers he receives. Obviously, then, it's important for a parent to have his own feelings sorted out as much as is possible before the questions come from his child.

The reflective ability of the school-aged child is growing, and the usual intense desire to be just like everyone else can make a child vulnerable to the criticism of other children, and harsh tongues are common in this age group.

The school-aged child who was adopted, including the child who was adopted transracially, may be unsure of himself at this stage, since his history and/or skin color are different from that of his friends. Unfortunately, his classmates, while they may have been born to their families, are experiencing similar feelings during this developmental stage, and this may be a time of teasing about differences. It certainly doesn't always happen, but if it does, it is important to remember the developmental basis of the focus.

A child whose skin color differs from that of his parents may find that the same friends who didn't seem to notice the difference during pre-school years might suddenly be questioning him or even teasing. Depending on personality and other factors, the child who was adopted may shrug off the teasing while another may be profoundly affected by it. Support from parents and teachers is critical at this time.

A number of changes take place in the mental development of the adolescent. He can, for example, for the first time, "think in terms of ideals and contrary-to-fact conditions." This ability has very important consequences for the young person as he thinks about the future, but also as he scrutinizes the present. It permits him to begin planning realistically for the future, a great step in maturation, but it is also the basis for a new perspective on the present—on his home, family, school, and community—for he can now compare them with his ideal version. When the adolescent does this, he often finds what he has sadly lacking in comparison with the ideal. This dissatisfaction can often become an issue of conflict between him and his parents.

Might the adolescent who was adopted, whether adopted by a family of the same race or transracially, also reevaluate his family and find it wanting in comparison with his ideal?

Vignettes in this section, "Looking Like Parents," are between parents and their children of all ages. At all developmental stages, these children fortunately were willing to discuss the differences that are evident to them as well as their varied feelings about differences.

❖

Janette: age three

"Janette is only three," said Suzie, the mother of a biological daughter Jenna, and Janette adopted transracially from India, "but even when she was two, she was identifying people according to skin colors! 'I am brown,' was one of her first sentences. 'What color is your dad, sweetie?' I asked. 'White.' 'And your sister?' 'White.' 'And your mother?' I couldn't wait to hear Janette's answer to that one because, as you can see, I'm quite olive in tone. And she got it! She said, 'Mostly brown.'

"Right now," Suzie said, "my husband and I feel it's important to acknowledge what Janette is noticing and not try to redirect her focus. It's okay to notice people's skin tones. Right now she seems to see only color. We'll see what she notices next."

"Believe me, her focus will change," laughed Jim, whose son Joseph the family adopted from Peru and who had just turned ten. "When Joseph was five, he was noticing hair colors. He said, 'I have dark hair. Daddy *used* to have dark hair!'"

❖

Looking Like Parents

Jeffrey: age three and one-half

"When I get big, can I get a haircut so my hair will look like Daddy's?" asked Cynthia's son Jeffrey, whose biracial heritage gave him curls even though his sister, also biracial, has very straight hair.

Cynthia felt that at his age Jeffrey's main desire as he asked this question was to be assured that he does in fact belong to his family and that the way he looks is perfect.

She answered, "I think your hair will always look just like it does now, Jeffrey. And I'm so glad. Do you know, I pay lots of money to make my hair look like your hair. Isn't it funny how we never seem to like the way our hair looks?"

Cynthia says she may be skirting the issue, and she knows when Jeffrey is five or six and older, their conversations about physical dissimilarities will be more pointed. Right now, though, her concern is that he feel good about himself and feel sure of his status in the family.

❖

Meggie: age four

Meggie is only four and therefore too young to understand these things, but she has asked more than once, "Mommy, when will my hair start looking like yours?"

Her mother Margherita's reply has always been, "Meggie, I love your hair just the way it is."

Since the question keeps being repeated, Margherita feels she must look more closely at it, however. She's prepared at the next query to say, "You wish you looked like Daddy and me. That's okay to wish. But we love the way you look."

Leigh, who has also adopted her children transracially, says she takes special pains to compliment her daughter's appearance, at times other than when the questions arise. She also, feeling that her nearly four-year-old daughter's questions at this point are reflecting the issue of "do I really belong?" more than "I look different than you," stresses things that she *does* do like her family, ways in which they *are* alike.

"Oh, when I was your age, I used to take my Oreo cookies apart before I ate them just like you do! We both like to jump rope! I didn't like spicy foods either when I was four," Leigh will say.

Leigh's husband has picked up on this, even though they happen never to have spoken of it. Without denying the differences in appearance, they are emphasizing, but not over-emphasizing, the similarities which they can easily find.

Margherita and Leigh agreed they must be truthful, that they would confuse their children if they in any way denied the differences in appearance in the families. But up through age four, it seemed so important to both of them that they first firmly establish that their children belong to their families. They knew they would deal more with differences in appearance in the future.

❖

Looking Like Parents

Jennie: age five

"What will I look like when I grow up?" Jennie asked.

Though the Powells had not met Jennie's birthmother in Peru, they had been told that she did not look at all like Jennie. Naomi really had nothing she could accurately pass on to her daughter.

"Well, it's too soon to tell," Naomi answered. She included Jennie's sister Molly, who is Caucasian, in the conversation at that point. They all stood in front of the mirror, Naomi's arms around her two daughters. "I never knew what I would look like, either. Molly looks a bit like me right now, doesn't she? And Jennie, you look quite a bit like Grandma B. who was tall and slim and used to have very black hair. It's going to be fun to watch, to see what you look like as you grow up. We're going to have to wait and see."

Naomi realized, however, that even though it's true no one knows exactly what he'll look like when he is grown, most people have some clues. It's probably something we take for granted if we were born into our families, she realized. And so she had to take seriously the concern on her daughters' part about how they would develop. Both are beautiful, but Naomi couldn't dismiss their questions with that observation.

It was her Hispanic daughter that most often questioned Naomi along these lines, but it was of concern also to her Caucasian daughter. She knew a bit more about Molly's birthparents, and so Naomi could tell her, "Your birthmother had reddish brown hair, and yours looks like it will be reddish brown, too."

Naomi realized how much the issue of resemblance meant to Jennie when she noticed a little girl on a television program. "Mom, look quick. That girl looks like me."

Indeed she did. Naomi and Jennie watched her and exclaimed about what a pretty girl she was and how Jennie could wear her hair like that, too.

Naomi thinks the comments and interest will continue. Her girls do not seem overly troubled by the subject, only curious and, perhaps, a bit wistful. Naomi will continue to listen and to offer what she can. Most of all, she will remain open to her daughters' inquiries and comments.

❖

Robby: age six

"And the man and woman who gave birth to you had beautiful brown skin just like yours, Robby. I wish Daddy's and my skin were just like yours, but it's lighter, isn't it? So we have different color skin, but we all love each other, don't we? And of course, that's what makes our family so terrific—how we feel about each other—not whether we look just like each other," Val explained to her six-year-old son.

"I want to be in our family. I just wish we were all the same," Robby sighed.

"Your life would have been different, wouldn't it, if your birthparents had been able to raise you or if you had been adopted by someone who had the same color skin as you. People stare at us so often, don't they? Why do you think they stare?" Val asked.

"Well, we're not like most families—except we're kind of like the Ingleses. Except they have three different colors in their family. I get mad at people when they stare. I want to smash them sometimes," Robby said heatedly.

"I feel angry, too, sometimes," Val responded. "I keep thinking people will get used to interracial families. There are lots of us, aren't there? And maybe they will get used to us sometime. But, do you know, sometimes I feel proud when people stare at us. Most of them seem friendly to me, just curious. And although they should know it's not polite to stare, I keep thinking 'They know we're an adoptive family. They know how much we all wanted each other. We're pretty neat.' ... And we are, you know."

"I guess. But it still makes me mad, Mommy."

"I understand. Tell me when it makes you mad, okay? We'll try to think of some way to handle it."

❖

Lynn: age six

"Why are your eyes funny? You don't look like your mom," was the first comment regarding her appearance that had confronted Stuart and Susan's daughter at school.

"I just told them I was born in Korea. My teacher showed everyone where Korea is on the big map. That was all," Lynn reported.

"Great. You helped educate the class!" Susan said enthusiastically. "Some day you might want to bring your Korean doll collection in to show everyone."

"Yeah, sometime." And Lynn was off to find her friends.

❖

David: age seven

"Kids can be mean when it comes to appearance," Katie said. Her son, whom she and Ronald had adopted from India at nine months of age, was seven now, and suddenly his skin color was an issue with his classmates. "They, of course, are at the stage where they are trying to decide what is okay."

"Ronald and I had always made information about India available to David, but now we doubled our efforts. We first gave him an 'answer' for his classmates comments: 'This is what people in my first country look like.' And then we proceeded to make him an expert, seven-year-old level, on India so that he was armed, I guess is the word. Why not wow them all with the Taj Mahal? Why not impress them with his knowledge of a country most knew little about?"

Ronald added, "And the mean comments did stop. Possibly they would have stopped anyway. But possibly David was less of a target as he grew in his knowledge, felt sure of himself, and was able to change the focus a bit with his assertions."

"Now this approach fits David's personality," Katie hastily added. "This isn't necessarily a solution for everyone, but it's an approach that is worth considering."

❖

John: age seven

"Perhaps it's just my own sensitivity," Carmen began, "but it seems my son has more racial comments addressed to him than do the other Hispanic children in our integrated community. Perhaps I'm just more attuned to what is said to my son. Perhaps other negative verbalizations are said to Hispanic kids who have Hispanic parents, too, when I'm not present.

"But I have this mother's instinct that tells me my son is singled out more often because his situation is unusual. He's a very brown-skinned Hispanic child with very fair-skinned Caucasian parents.

"I have tried to improve the situation whenever he tells me about something that has happened or when I hear it first hand. I've jumped into conversations with none-too-subtle analogies of how nice differences are—in foods, in games, in people. I've talked about how much more interesting it makes the world, about the monotony we would face if everything and everyone were alike. When a classmate said, 'I don't want to play with you because you're brown,' I talked to his teachers. I've sent notes when appropriate to keep teachers informed.

"What I hope, of course, is that John will be comfortable with the fact that we are an interracial family. I see many good signs that he is. The other day, in fact, he defended himself when another comment about his

76

brown skin came his way. I was driving the car pool, and I heard one little boy say to my son, 'You can't sit by the window because you're brown.'

John shot back, "No, you can't sit by the window because you have red hair."

"At that point both boys began laughing, and I left it alone. I'm not sure if anything was learned in the exchange, but it gave me comfort to realize my son can take care of himself and can maintain a sense of humor, which will always be a valuable asset. I was pleased that John didn't crumple, nor did he feel he should 'just take it,' nor did he give way to unnecessary anger. Instead he asserted himself appropriately.

"Self-esteem? I don't think we have to worry about his!"

❖

Paige: age seven

The Barretts had adopted Paige as an infant and had always had a hard time convincing people that she was not their biological child. Her skin tone, her eye color, her hair, were exactly like her mom's.

Paige was seven before Scott, also blond and fair-skinned, but brown-eyed, joined their family. Paige quickly became the doting big sister. She picked out Scott's outfits every day. She helped with the bottle.

One day as Paige sat holding her brother and gazing at him adoringly, she said, "Mom, can you change the color of a baby's eyes?"

"I don't think so," Monica answered. "Why do you ask?"

"Well, if Scotty's eyes were blue, he'd look like our family."

"Are you thinking it would be nice if we all looked alike?" Monica asked.

Paige nodded.

"Oh, sweetheart, you really love that little brother of yours, don't you?" Monica responded, reading Paige's concern between the lines. "You want to be sure he knows he belongs to our family, don't you?"

Again Paige nodded.

"And people always say how much you look like me, and nobody says that when they look at Scotty, do they? They just say how cute he is, don't they?"

"I just don't want him to feel bad," Paige ventured.

"Of course, sometimes kids don't look alike even if they were born into their families. Remember your Uncle Jeff? Well, he and your Daddy are brothers, you know. And Uncle Jeff is short and has brown hair. And Daddy is tall and blond."

"Uncle Jeff is Daddy's brother?" Paige asked, seemingly as amazed at figuring out that relationship as she was at realizing how different those biological brothers were.

"And guess what. It didn't matter in the family if they looked alike or not. If a family cares for each other and helps each other and has a good time together—I think that's what makes it a neat family."

78

Monica waited, wondering if there was more to say. Was Paige also concerned about whether she herself would have been loved as much if she hadn't looked so much like the family? Monica decided to tuck that topic away for another day as she joined Paige and Scott on the floor.

"Hmm," Monica finally mused, "how do you think we could be sure Scotty knows he's part of our family when he gets older?"

"Well," Paige answered, "we could tell him about Daddy and Uncle Jeff."

❖

Romondo and Carlos: ages seven and eight

"We adopted our sons from Colombia at ages seven and eight. Socially they are such individuals. One has a small group of close friends, all of them Caucasian. The other seems to fit in anywhere and has a wide range of friends from different ethnic groups. Their differences seem personality related. The one with the wide group of friends is very easy going and gregarious; the other is more reserved."

"How about your relationship with the boys?" Sheila asked.

"I have good relationships with both my sons, luckily," Kathleen said. "But it is interesting, and I've talked about this with people who are considering transracial adoption. They often ask about 'bonding.' Some who phone me are afraid of not being able to bond with a child that looks different than them.

"My experience, though, was that the easier, quicker bonding happened to be with the child who was most different from me in appearance, the one with the darker skin tone."

"Kids are individuals and we mustn't stereotype. That's the lesson, isn't it?"

❖

Jimmy and Jeffrey: ages seven and nine

Patricia and Clark's interracial family was a step more complex than many since their children were biracial as well, born to Caucasian and African-American birthparents. The whole family happened to love experimenting with new foods, both the cooking and the eating aspects, and so Patricia and Clark had chosen this avenue, foods of Africa, to educate their children about that part of their heritage.

They had chosen a nicely integrated community in which to live. School had been relatively smooth for the children until recently. But now Jimmy, age seven, was coming home on occasion with hurt feelings and concerns about being different. And then Jeffrey, age nine, perhaps defensively, uttered a disparaging remark about Asians at the dinner table one evening.

The tack Patricia and Clark took was to try to help their sons appreciate *all* differences, hoping they would in the process embrace their own as well as those of Asian and other classmates. "We expanded our experimentation with foods to those of other countries and continents. The meals would inevitably lead to discussions about each country, which we first located on the ever-handy globe. We would look up bits of information in reference books," Clark explained. "Every culture seemed to have something fascinating and inviting about it to the children. We've fantasized as a family about visiting many of them."

Will this approach suceed? Some of the discussions give Patricia and Clark hope. Differences are hard for children to accept, especially at certain developmental levels, and appreciating the differences is the key. Objective exposure, through whatever medium, seems to this family to be a positive way to educate the children to rise above these concerns.

❖

Christina: age eight

"Being an interracial family has for us been a wonderful and broadening experience, although I think I might add that if you feel any reservations about becoming such a family, I don't advise it for you," Rosalind began.

"Our family has made an adventure of learning about the foods of Korea, the customs, the clothing. One disappointment on my part is that I didn't think far enough ahead when we were in Korea. I purchased clothing for my new daughter who was a toddler, as well as for her older sister who had stayed in the states with her aunt and uncle, but I didn't look ahead to their growing up and wanting to show these costumes to their friends and schoolmates. I wish I had bought more.

"Being an interracial family has helped us make choices about our lifestyle. We've made a point of fostering friendships with many families of different races and in fact purposely live in a very integrated neighborhood.

"My children are often questioned by their friends who are curious about racial differences in a single family. My older daughter, who is Caucasian, takes over for the younger one when they are asked, 'Are you sisters?'"

"Yes," says Christina, "this is my sister. She's from Korea. She's adopted."

And then the next inevitable question is, "Are you adopted, too?"

Christina answers "Yes" and at this point seems to feel obligated to do more explaining. Rosalind can sense that she's getting weary of the questioning. It may be time to tell Christina that, unless she feels like it, lengthy explanations are not necessary.

The son of Rosalind's friend has a polite but terse reply when asked, "Is that your brother?" He matter-of-factly answers, "Yes." Period.

❖

Janet: age eight

"My daughter, Janet, whom we adopted in Peru, has never talked much about the interracial aspect of our family. She knows as much as we know about her year in Peru. She has seen all the pictures and the souvenirs of our trip," Libby said.

"Nor does she talk about being racially different from most of her friends. She has a solid little group of neighborhood girl friends at school, and since they have grown up together and are accustomed to each other and stick together, the topic simply doesn't seem to come up.

82

"I happen to have an Hispanic colleague in my office complex who expressed an interest in meeting Janet. I jumped at the opportunity to supply my daughter with such a delightful role model: a female minority professional who happened to have been born in a country bordering Peru.

"It's become a bit of a ritual for me to bring Janet to the office on one or two of her school holidays each year. She'll spend most of her day helping me, but we'll always find some reason for her to be in my colleague's office for a time.

"My ulterior motives remain unspoken. Perhaps the process will become verbalized in time, perhaps not. Janet's learning style is essentially an imitative one. She watches and learns. I know she's learning by observing my colleague. At this time, I think that's all that is needed for Janet."

❖

Jared: age eight

For nearly two years, Sherri and Stan, who had adopted Jared as an infant in Peru, listened and commiserated while he talked about the interracial aspect of their family. His comments always contained some form of "I wish I looked like you" or "I wish you looked like me."

Fortunately Jared was having another good year at school. He had three close friends, and the four boys drifted from one backyard to the next every day after school. The emphasis about differences, then, was not coming from his classmates. It was Jared's own concern.

Stan and Sherri decided to take a new look at the concept since Jared's comments were beginning to sound more like habit than actual concern. In addition, while they were not denying that the differences were a reality and had to be discussed, they finally realized that every such exchange left them feeling slightly guilty and unsure. "Did we do him a disservice by removing him from 'his country'?" was the core question.

Stan explained, "We finally realized that the alternative, namely that we wouldn't have been a family, was unthinkable. We decided to quit wishing for some perfect world, and enjoy the one we have, and enjoy being an interracial family."

Sherri added, "It's not as if we trivialize Jared's feelings. But since we have talked about it in depth many times, we are now saying, in effect, 'Yes, that would be nice, wouldn't it?' We are agreeing with him—and then just going on as if he'd said he wished he lived in Boston or had a pony.

"If the occasion or the tone of voice seems to warrant it, we'll certainly talk about it as much as Jared would like to. But we're trying to convey to him that this is not the end of the world. That we're glad we're a family. We want him to know that *this* feeling supersedes any concern, any worry, about whether transracial adoption is perfect."

❖

Maite: age eight

"Maite, whom we adopted as an infant, not only looks like our family, but she *acts* like us, too," Jeanne began. "She has my laugh and her dad's mannerisms while she talks, and talk she does—like our whole family!

"The change in her approach to talking about adoption during the past few months has been so interesting. We've been traveling a great deal as a family, and so we have met scores of new people. Since Maite is such a little card, it's almost inevitable that someone will make a remark about her appearance or actions. 'You look just like your mom.' 'You are so much like your mom.'

"Up until last year, Maite would have informed the crowd early on about the fact that she was adopted. But recently, she's become discriminating about whether or not she discloses this fact. I've noticed that, if she's not necessarily the center of attention and someone says, 'You look just like your mom,' Maite will just smile and say 'Thank you.' If, on the other hand, she is indeed the center of attention, she is more likely to talk about her adoption. She'll say, 'Thank you, and isn't it funny, because I was adopted.'

"She's always rewarded with 'Amazing' or 'Incredible', or 'You're kidding,' and we see her eyes twinkle in enjoyment. In other words, she's comfortable explaining her adoption or not, as it suits her purposes. We think it's great. That's the attitude we hoped she'd have."

❖

Chip, Amy and John: ages six, seven, nine

Marilyn and Dave adopted three children, each of whom has one African-American birthparent and one Caucasian. Their children are physically very dissimilar, one having straight brown hair and olive skin. "I chuckle, by the way, when people actually argue with me and insist that John is in fact Hispanic!" Marilyn says.

85

"My daughter, who is very light skinned, came home from school quite upset recently," Marilyn continued. "The children were painting self-portraits in art class, and my daughter, in an attempt to be accurate, had said she was 'black and white' and had asked for help with the coloring. She received no help because her teacher, with whom I shall have to have a chat, didn't believe her.

"My older son, whose skin is a darker brown, seems to be the one who is least sure of where he 'fits' socially. I see him drift between groups of classmates. At the moment he seems closer to African-American friends. Last year it was his Caucasian friends.

"I'm not saying any of this is a large problem. I'm simply saying there is an additional level of complexity to being an interracial family.

"We are, first of all, a regular and a happy family. We feel our children each bonded with us and with each other early and firmly. Now, as they venture out into the world of school, situations arise and will continue to arise because of this interracial fact. My husband and I will be there to listen and understand and guide when we can."

❖

Ben: age ten

Ben, who resembled his parents to a great extent, had asked about the ethnicity of his birthparents when he was quite young and had learned that he was of Irish descent. That fact seemed important to Ben, and he would, with his family's help, celebrate St. Patrick's Day and generally wear lots of green.

One evening at the dinner table Ben asked, "Could I have the potatoes, please?"

Surprised, his father answered, "Here they are, but I didn't know you liked them."

Ben answered, "Well, I never did, but I just realized something. Since I'm Irish, I really ought to be getting into potatoes!"

❖

Phillip: age twelve

It took Eva and her family a while to come up with the perfect answer.

One of her children was adopted domestically and is Caucasian. The other two are both from Peru, but one is light skinned and one quite a bit darker in tone. Perhaps the three different skin tones made their family especially susceptible to intrusive questioning. Strangers would routinely come up and ask, "Where are you all from?"

Phillip, only twelve at the time, finally thought of it. "Let's tell them we're all from here," he said, laughing. "Let's tell them we're all from Chicago!"

❖

Caroline: age fourteen

"My daughter actually resembled my baby pictures when she was an infant," Dawn said. "And so our looking alike as a family was never an issue when she was small. And since my husband is tall and we all have much the same coloring, our looking alike is still not an issue to the outside world."

"But Caroline is tall, and you're so small," ventured Tess. "I'll bet it's a concern with her—just as it is with my daughter."

"I'd give anything for her long legs," Dawn laughed. "But Caroline thinks she's too tall, her feet are too long, and her bones are too big. It's so bittersweet, because while I'm thrilled that she's identified with me to the extent that she wants to be like me, I'm so concerned about her feeling good about herself."

"I know exactly what you mean," Tess responded. "A friend of mine, who realized her daughter would be very tall, enrolled her in modeling school where her height was an advantage."

"I tried that," Dawn said, "but my daughter likes sports instead. So, we've encouraged sports, and that is helping Caroline feel capable and accomplished. She's a wonderful volleyball player with her height and athletic ability, and she's becoming a very good tennis player as well."

"It's so ironic," Tess continued, "because both our daughters are so beautiful. Of course, it's often hard for an adolescent girl to realize that about herself. Adolescents want to be just like everyone else and not stand out in the crowd. So, it's easy for a girl whose mom is short to feel that she'd rather not be taller than most of her friends."

Dawn agreed and added, "I wonder which is the real issue—not looking like us or not blending in size-wise with their friends. Something tells me it's being different than friends that bothers them more, but probably it's a combination."

"I'm rethinking one thing I've been doing," Dawn said. "I've in essence been putting myself down in an attempt to make Caroline feel better about herself. I say I wish I were taller, that I'm too thin, that my hair has never been thick like hers. And of course it isn't working. What Caroline needs is to feel good about her uniqueness even while I feel good about mine. There are so many different ways a person can look and still be attractive."

"What can help any adolescent value himself or herself?" Tess asked rhetorically. "Probably the dozens of little positive comments and valid observations we as parents make will eventually be heard. Probably just the maturing process will help. In the meantime, we must remember the adolescent years are rough for so many young people—not just the ones who were adopted. We mustn't make the mistake of thinking every adolescent girl born to her family is perfectly delighted with her body! Parents can find scores of reasons to feel guilty if they've a mind to. Let's just not feel guilty about being short!"

❖

Juan: age fourteen

"The waiter in the Peruvian restaurant, who was still struggling to learn English, was clearly delighted to see my son at our table," Diana said. "You could just see him expecting to be able to communicate easily with Juan, whom we adopted at age three from Peru."

"My son has lost most of the Spanish that he knew as a young child, and of course he speaks English with no accent. The waiter's look changed, and so did Juan's."

Juan is not a young man who communicates readily about his feeling, but it wasn't hard for Diana to read what was going through his mind. "I don't belong with the waiter, who looks like me, and I don't really belong with my family, either."

Diana realized that this marked a new phase for her son. He would be more independent, going most places without her from now on. He needed to understand the dynamics of what had just occurred.

"That was really awkward, wasn't it?" Diana said to Juan. "He thought you'd be speaking Spanish."

Diana knew her son well enough to realize he probably wouldn't contribute to the conversation, but she felt it was important to say it, and that Juan would appreciate the confirmation of his feelings.

She was rewarded with a smile, however, when she said, "It was nice to be with you and feel at home in this neighborhood, though. See—there are some advantages to having different skin tones in one family!"

❖

Carlos and Robert: teens

When the Farrs traveled to Colombia to meet their younger son, they decided to purchase a number of ceremonial items while there: a typical tablecloth, a candelabra that would be used for certain celebrations. "We researched the holidays and chose the most meaningful," Carla said. "As a family we've learned a lot as we've attempted to duplicate the appropriate customs.

"In this and other ways we have attempted to keep Carlos' culture alive in our family. Of course, he is an American, but we want to give him familiarity with the culture of his birth as well.

"We were a bit concerned that these rituals might cause jealousy on the part of our older son, Robert, whom we had adopted domestically. To solve that, we decided to emphasize his ethnicity as well. Since his birthparents both happened to be from Irish families, we chose the obvious and have always celebrated St. Patrick's Day as his.

"We feel it's important not to overdo any of this. We want our children primarily to feel they are our children. But we have chosen something extra and wonderful about each of them to celebrate as well."

❖

Anthony: age fifteen

Anthony was in fact Hispanic, but he had been associating with the African-American community during the entire school year. He liked sports. His new friends were also good athletes. He liked dancing and was good at it. So were his friends.

As Anthony rode along with his Caucasian mother in the family station wagon one afternoon, the words on the rap radio station suddenly became too vulgar for Trish to ignore. She looked at her fifteen-year-old son, knowing he wouldn't like what she had to say. "I have to change the station. I'm not comfortable with that song."

"Well," Anthony rejoined, "if you were black, you wouldn't object."

"Well," said Trish, "I'm not black. But if I were, I'm not sure I would like this anyway—and here's why."

The conversation, mostly one-sided, went on as Trish talked about feminism and using people and violence. She'd certainly been right that Anthony wouldn't care for her interference, but she hadn't guessed that he would voice his displeasure by referring to the fact that they were an interracial family. "Eek," Trish thought. "This is how kids tell us what's on their minds."

Anthony's fantasy was that *black* moms all over the country could be found cooking dinner and listening to rap music.

And of course there was also the embarrassing fact of being fifteen, not quite old enough to drive. Having *Mom* drive you to and from practice was humiliating. Let's put a bit of distance between mom and son. Let's tell her she's not quite with it.

Trish smiled.

❖

Roberto: teen

Susan's son was a light-skinned Colombian boy, light-skinned as many Colombian's are. But the stereotype in this country of the South Amerian person is one of a darker skin tone. And so Roberto, who was adopted as an eight-year-old and had strong ties to Colombia, was often met with disbelief when he talked about the country of his birth.

Roberto often dated Caucasian girls, and their parents would frequently respond "No!" in disblief when he mentioned his birthplace. "It wasn't necessarily that he felt they were being negative or biased," Susan said. "It just felt to him that they were denying him his heritage." Since he felt so connected to Colombia, he talked about it often, and so this conversation was not uncommon. He felt he needed to defend his right to be himself.

"That defensive quality to his answers reminds me of myself when Roberto's sister was small," Susan offered. "We adopted her from Colombia as a one-year-old, and often, on our grocery-store outings, people would ask me if she were my daughter. I never just left it at 'Yes.' I always felt a need to defend her right to be here—I guess it was.

"Now Roberto is defending himself. It's okay. I wish it didn't have to be, but he's handling it.

"I encourage Roberto to look at himself as a 'ground breaker.' To think of himself as educating people about Colombia, since that is in fact what he is doing. And then the next child who comes here from Colombia will not have to do as much educating.

"I'm not saying every child should need to feel that he is an ambassador from his country of birth, but since Roberto has chosen this role, I'm attempting to help him to view what he is doing not as an ordeal but as a contribution. It's the difference between his just reacting to something that doesn't feel right—and having a cause. There's strength and purpose in a cause, and I hope this point of view will help my son avoid bitterness or cynicism."

❖

Looking Like Parents

John: age seventeen

John, whom his parents had adopted from India, had always talked openly about adoption, brought friends home readily, and using the delightful sense of humor that helped make him the endearing son he was, would introduce his "pale parents" to his friends. Conversations about adoption would quite often ensue after such a presentation.

On one particular night, the group was meeting at John's house before the game, and John was to drive them all in the van. There were some new boys in the group.

"Do you want to bring them in to say hello before you go?" Will and Mary asked.

John thought for a moment, and then said, "Not tonight. It would take too long."

Mary and Will knew what he meant. They all laughed.

❖

Thomas: age seventeen

"Are you sure it's okay for us to come to your soccer game?" Lynn teased her son. "Not so long ago you wouldn't let us come within miles of the field!"

"Now, Mom, that was two whole years ago," Thomas rejoined. "I've grown up. And besides that, you and Dad have improved a lot recently," he teased in return.

And then thoughtfully, Thomas added, "Actually it was kind of hard, though, before I could drive. Every time you'd drop me off at practice, I figured the guys were thinking, 'Oh, yeah, he's adopted,' whenever they'd look into the car and see your white face after looking at me with my brown skin. Adoption was okay. It's just that I didn't like being reminded of it at every practice. I had other things to think about."

Thomas laughed. "Aren't you glad I'm so mature now?"

❖

Cathryn: teen

"Seth and I were told Cathryn's birthmother was quite tall," Brenda explained, " and Cathryn's lovely, lanky legs indicate she may be fortunate enough to be tall as well. Cathryn's and my coloring is much the same, and since Seth is tall, it's not obvious that we are an adoptive family.

"Families built through interracial adoption are more readily evident and many have developed strategies for dealing with comments and questions of strangers. While our situation is probably easier, it's not without its complications.

"A chatty stranger will occasionally offer 'You look just like your mom.' My daughter and I have an unspoken strategy for these times," Brenda continued. "We simply smile at each other."

❖

Adult to adult

As the new family built by adoption strolled along the beach at dusk while vacationing in the Bahamas, the Caucasian couple and their Asian infant passed two of the local young men of the island. The young men did a slight double take upon encountering the family. After they had passed each other, but not out of earshot, one young man said to the other, "Hey, mon, those folks got the wrong baby!"

"The tone was so positive and fun-filled that we just laughed," Joe said. "Certainly the statement showed an awareness of the racial differences in our family, but not a negative feeling about it."

Ruth added, "How can people not be aware of differences? That doesn't mean they disapprove. I understand that harsh things are said to inter-racial families at times, and we'll deal with that if it should happen."

Ruth's friend Sonia chimed in, "What matters to Russ and me is how our friends treat us once they are used to the difference. We've gotten only respect and caring. Our girls are in school now, and all's well. I'm not saying negative things can't happen, but so far it's been great."

A Caucasian mother who had lived during the past fifteen years in several different countries agreed. "When we lived in Venezuela, everyone noticed our daughter, whom we adopted from Colombia. Certainly the Venezuelans noticed, but it was definitely with approval. Comments would be made about how lucky our daughter was. We always responded that we were the lucky ones."

A Danish woman whose son was also born in Colombia had a similar experience. "When we vacationed in Cozumel, the swimming pool was filled with children from all over the world. We were living in the U.S. at the time, and when my son was asked where he was from, he responded, 'We're living in New York right now.' When questioned further, he said, 'I'm Danish.' And that was the end of it. Ahh, don't we wish the whole world could be as sophisticated and non-provincial in its outlook as that swimming pool full of children!"

Looking Like Parents

Adult to adult

Grandma and Grandpa were in town on the occasion of their second-grade granddaughter's class play. A mom, who obviously was unaware that Phyllis and her husband had adopted their daughter, was being kind and conversational to the visiting grandparents.

"Your granddaughter looks just like you," she said to the grandmother.

Grandma was caught by surprise and simply turned and looked at Phyllis questioningly. "Say 'Thank you,' Mom," Phyllis smiled.

"My rule-of-thumb is this," Phyllis explained later to Grandma. "If the person who inadvertently brings up the subject of adoption is someone with whom I am likely to have an on-going relationship, I am most comfortable if I pursue the subject right at that time. I might have said in the above situation, for instance, 'Oh, don't we love that, Mom? We don't get to take any biological credit for it, though. Jack and I adopted Cynthia when she was tiny.'

"I'm always ready with additional conversation," Phyllis added, "because I find that kind of statement often leaves the person speechless for a few moments. My continued chatting will give the person the chance to formulate a reply and removes any feeling of awkwardness on anyone's part.

"If the person, on the other hand, is a stranger and will probably remain so—another parent watching our son's basketball game, for example—I never feel that I have any obligation to be sure this parent understands our family's history. I simply smile in such a case and say the obvious. 'Thank you.'"

❖

Looking Like Parents

Adult to adult

"Our two daughters were born to us," Barbara began, "and they couldn't be more different from each other. Our two sons we adopted from Peru, and they couldn't be more different from each other."

"It makes you wonder if environment has anything at *all* to do with how a child 'turns out'! I'm exaggerating," Lynn assured Barbara. "But it does make you feel children are pretty much born with personalities."

"My sons from Peru illustrate that," Barbara added. "They were six and eight when we adopted them, and so they both have memories of their culture. One has his room jammed with Peruvian flags and other mementos. The other just isn't that interested.

"And both seem content with their ways of dealing with their heritage. It's not like the one seems to be avoiding it or the other seems consumed by it.

"We've tried to be open to talking about Peru. We'll bring up items of interest from the news, for example. We don't overemphasize it, but we make it available. And each boy has responded in his own way.

"I feel good about the way each has developed, and I think there's a lesson in our experience. Each child should be allowed to respond in his own way to his heritage, and we as parents shouldn't worry about that response.

"We also shouldn't assume that children will be consistent in their feelings over time. Another child I know wanted nothing to do with India, the country of his birth, until his late teens. He may lose some of his present keen interest once his questions are answered, and he may not. Either way, it's okay."

Adult to adult

"I often hear it secondhand," Victoria explained as she discussed comments that come their way as an interracial family. "And then I can't do anything about it.

"I almost prefer people just saying it to me, and then I can discuss it with them. Even if the children are there, they are old enough now to recognize bias when they hear it. And I'd just as soon they hear me refute that bias we encounter. Then if they are alone and a comment is made, I don't think it will be quite as devastating as if they'd never heard me handle it.

"Our children are Asian, and it's amazing how often people take it upon themselves to let me know that they think these children should have 'stayed with their own people.' With thinly disguised racism, others will express 'concern' for my children, asserting that they surely would have been better off in 'their own country.'

"It took me a while to formulate my replies, but I decided to try to educate people rather than simply get furious. I explain now that there is no adoption in the country where my children were born. I explain that a child is better off being in a family than in an orphanage or on the street.

"I'm usually met with blank stares, granted, and then the people hurry on. Some appear to be thoughtful, however. How many will think twice before approaching another interracial family is something I can't predict. I can only hope.

"Now you've heard how I handle intrusions on my *good* days!" Victoria continued. "I'm not a saint, and sometimes I get irritated by the rudeness. However, I try to remember that many people *are* curious about interracial families, and curiousity isn't always negative, even though the comments I've just cited are.

"Most often interest on the part of strangers takes a more benign bent. As with the hostile comments, I feel that I can choose how to answer or whether to answer. If I feel like using the moment as an opportunity to teach, I will do so. If it feels merely intrusive to me at the time, I can list, as all of us can, any number of ways to avoid conversation and extricate myself.

"I'm trying to treat rude people as people who just don't understand. I hope that is a healthy attitude for my children to assimilate. I hope it will keep them from feeling bitter or victimized. Ignorance on the part of people can only be handled by education, and this is what we will try in our small way to accomplish."

❖

Adult to adult

"I would never presume," Judy began, "to choose between Caucasian or African American, to declare one or the other as the racial identity of my children. And yet this is what forms at schools and even the Government Census forms ask you to do. And so I leave them blank."

"I understand support groups of interracial families are lobbying to change these insensitive forms. All that is needed is a line that says 'biracial,' and everyone would be comfortable.

"What is reflected in these forms is the denial on the part of society of the very identity of some of its members. My children are biracial.

They should not have to declare themselves to be 'other.' And if they are required to choose and declare one heritage, they are, in fact, forced to deny the other.

"People are who they are, and it's okay, and that this could be accepted is the ideal attitude for society."

❖

Adult to adult

"We enthusiastically became an interracial family when we adopted our sons from Korea. It introduced us to another culture, something my husband and I relished from the start," Eve said.

"Our parents, while initially happy for us but slightly skeptical that they themselves could feel a kinship with a culture so different from their own, have become very involved as well. They'll clip newspaper articles about Korea or dig out a wonderful old *National Geographic* about Asia. We're forever grateful that they have taken it upon themselves to make scrapbooks about Korea, two identical ones, which we know our sons will treasure someday.

"It's been thrilling to watch the grandparents grow. Their initial attachment to both our children was, I might add, instantaneous. How could anyone resist!

"Not everything is perfect in our extended family, however," Eve continued. "One sister-in-law professes to love our children 'like a real part of the family since they were raised like Americans.' At the same time she's condescendingly sweet to another niece who was born in Cambodia to my brother-in-law and his Cambodian wife. They lived in

Cambodia and Thailand for several years before coming to the United States, and so their daughter was not 'raised like an American.'

"We will keep attempting over the years to emphasize our interest in our cultural diversity and at the same time give attention to our similarities as peoples. We hope someday our sister-in-law will learn to appreciate people for whom they are. If not, I'm afraid it's her loss."

❖

Adult to adult

Judy and Mike, both Caucasian, domestically adopted Mark, a biracial infant with African-American and Caucasian birthparents.

"I soon realized," Judy said, "that the questions and comments and looks directed at us were different when the three of us were together than they were when my son and I were by ourselves.

"When you're not with Mark and me," she had told Mike, "people assume ours is an interracial marriage, which is fine with me.

"It soon occurred to me," Judy continued, "that our being comfortable with interracial marriage was crucial. If we were uncomfortable with interracial marriage, we would in fact be saying we were uncomfortable with our child's biological heritage.

"I might be going out on a limb here," Judy continued, "but I'm going to make that an even stronger statement. It's my opinion that unless a person is comfortable with interracial marriage, that person should not adopt a biracial child."

❖

Adult to adult

Mary said she was speaking just for herself, but she didn't think she, as a Caucasian parent, could as easily give her minority children, in this case African-American children, the skills to cope with racism that an African-American parent could. Which simply meant she had some extra work to do.

"I talk with my African-American friends endlessly," she said. "They are very helpful and usually have a similar anecdote about a situation that their own children have faced.

"I am honest with my children about the problem as well," she continued. "I say, 'I haven't lived with it. I can hurt for you—but I don't know how it is.'

"I tell my children the stories told to me by other parents. We're slowly learning together.

"Don't get me wrong. We are a happy and healthy and stable family, and this is not an apology. It's simply an awareness that there is something with which I can use help."

❖

Adult to adult

"A pet peeve of mine, or maybe it's stronger that that, is the way our society wants to have us all in tidy little boxes. 'Is she your daughter?' people will ask about my Korean-born child. I know we look different, but with international adoption so common, I keep wondering when people will simply *assume* she's my daughter," Linnea said heatedly.

"I make a point of pointing us out, as it were," Elizabeth said. "When Tory and I are shopping, for instance, I'll say to the clerk, 'I don't know if my daughter will like this. I'll have to check with her.' Then when Tory joins me, there's no question about our relationship. I hope this helps to get people used to families with differences.

"A little education. I think that's what it will take. I hope that's what it will take."

❖

Adult to adult

Shirley and Hank wished they could live in an integrated community since they had adopted their children transracially. It just didn't work out that way, however. Hank's transfer to a small town in the midwest was mandatory if he was to remain with the company, and there weren't many jobs to he found at the moment.

Besides, it was a wonderful opportunity for the children to experience a non-city environment. The schools were good. The people were nice. Everyone seemed accepting of the interracial family with Caucasian parents and Asian children.

Hank said, "We heard of International Reunions held yearly for families who have adopted children from various Asian countries. We decided we would make a habit of incorporating a Reunion into our summer plans."

They also heard of ethnic summer camps the children could attend when they were a bit older. This would give them a rather intensive exposure to children with backgrounds similar to their own. Summer vacations would include visiting other interracial families when possible.

Shirley added, "It might not be perfect, but we decided to look at the positive side of the situation. This is a pretty good solution. And what in life is perfect, anyway."

❖

Adult to adult

"I don't know how many phone calls I've gotten," Jane began. "It may be a complete stranger given my number by a mutual friend. Often the woman—it's usually a woman—is in tears. She will say she and her husband want desperately to adopt transracially, but they have reason to believe their families won't be very accepting of their children.

"My answer has remained the same from day one. I do some sincere commiserating about how difficult it is, and then I say what I believe to be the hard truth: A couple must be willing to cut off their families if the families can't accept their children.

"That said, I can be slightly encouraging. We were initially worried about my husband's family, but they came through!

"People often surprise you. People often grow. But some don't, and if that should be the sad case, a couple must be prepared to remove themselves from a family that would hurt their children. Their first responsibility is to their nuclear family, their children and themselves. Anything positive that might develop beyond that has to be viewed as a precious gift."

Adult to adult

"We are going to adopt a child from South America," Karen told her parents. She and Phillip had adopted their son domestically three years earlier, and so adoption was not new to the family. But transracial adoption was.

Karen held her breath for a moment, but her parents came through. "Good," they both said, nodding their heads.

It wasn't exactly an exuberant response, but at least it was a positive one.

The happy ending to the story is that Karen's parents have become her children's biggest fans. They are at the swim meets and the baseball games. They drop by to take their grandchildren to the donut shop or the ice cream parlor. The mutual adoration shows on every face.

The slightly hesitant beginning has given way to ringing endorsement.

❖

Chapter Five

Combination Families

Parents in "combination families," current terminology for those containing children born into their families as well as children adopted into their families, sometimes have concerns about whether the dual methods of entering the family are indeed of concern to their children. Some parents feel they themselves vascillate, worrying perhaps too much first about the children adopted by them and next about the children born to them.

Many find that close attention to developmental stages of children helps alleviate some concern as they observe both adopted and biological children handle the successive stages, sometimes perhaps with different emphases, but essentially similarly.

The preschool child's primary attachment is to his parents. His job during these early childhood years is to separate, to differentiate himself somewhat from his parents, to become his own person, but only to a point. The preschool child is, after all, still nearly totally dependent upon his parents. The parental task during these years is to help children feel secure even while they become their own persons.

The school-aged child, adopted or born into his family, wants to be just like everyone else. In the important ways, being loved and belonging to the family, these siblings are exactly alike. But there is a difference, namely the methods of entering the family, that may and probably should surface and be dealt with during these years.

School-aged children, developing skills rapidly, discover talents and strengths and weaknesses in themselves. The parent in the combination family, perhaps more than many parents, has in front of him the reminder that each child, adopted or born into the family, is in fact his own person. The parent's awareness of the development of children adopted into the family, and about whom he harbors no genetic expectations, can remind him that the child born to him is, also, a unique individual who may have inherited his parent's traits or may not have. He might feel that the best advice he can give parents in combination families, or any parents, is to view each child as special, knowing that a child, any child, deserves to have parents that value his uniqueness.

While adoption and birth may be common topics of thought and conversation in combination families during children's school-aged years, if a child becomes obsessed about adoption, it probably means there are other problems with which the family should deal.

The adolescent, who has in the past generally viewed his parents and siblings with affection, continues to do so, but now begins to look at them with a more critical eye. During early adolescence, it is hard for parents to be considered acceptable under any circumstances.

Siblings also come under new scrutiny at this time. The young adolescent feels closer to older siblings than to younger ones. Younger ones are viewed as a nuisance; older ones are emulated.

During adolescence then, the young person begins to look at his home and family with the eyes of an outside observer. He is consumed with making an impression and with how other people will react to his home and family, and so he may become hypercritical. Might the adolescents in combination families be reacting in similar ways to parents and siblings? Might the adopted or "born into" status of siblings be one, but only one, of the contentions at this stage?

108

The variety of stories in this chapter ranges from the bondings to the insecurities felt among siblings in combination families.

❖

Hannah: age five

"But why didn't I grow in your tummy like Brandon did?" Hannah asked her mother.

Cheryl and Will had carefully explained to Hannah the two methods by which she and Brandon had entered their family. Obviously she was now beginning to understand.

"Mommy and I wanted a baby very much, honey," Will began. "When we went to the doctor, he said it might be very hard to get a baby to grow in Mommy's tummy, that it might be a long time before that happened.

"And so then Mommy and I had a choice to make. We could have waited and waited and wondered whether a baby would ever grow in Mommy's tummy, or we could have adopted a child. Guess what we decided?"

"You adopted *me*," Hannah said with pride in her voice.

"That's right!" Cheryl said, leaving out at this point in time the waiting they had endured before Hannah was placed in their arms. "And we're *so* glad we did. We were so excited when we knew you could come home with us to be our daughter forever."

"And then we were pretty surprised and happy when we found out that Brandon was growing in Mommy's tummy," Will continued. "We were so happy that we'd have *two* children. We think we're very lucky to have been able to adopt one child and have one child born to us. We couldn't have been more excited about either you or Brandon coming into our family."

❖

Bobby: age six

Peter and Carol felt their agency had done a wonderful job of preparing them for international adoption. And so important to them was their feeling that the agency had also been careful to include Bobby, their six-year-old biological son, in their education. Peter and Carol and Bobby looked upon the adoption as a family venture, and so did the agency.

"They were aware of the need for the siblings to bond—as well as the parents and child," Peter said appreciatively. "We were glad all three of us could make the trip to Peru."

Carol added, "The most touching thing happened when we got to the orphanage. They were waiting for us, brought Lia into the room, and they put her first into Bobby's arms!"

❖

April: age six

April, adopted as an infant, had just turned six when her baby brother was born into the Price family. April's understanding of adoption, and then of birth, was quite thorough for a child of her age. She had always asked questions about everything, including adoption.

She had asked about her birthmother, especially during her mother's pregnancy, and Faith and her husband carefully told her that her birthmother didn't think she could be a good parent at that time in her life. That they were sure her birthmother loved her, but that she didn't feel old enough to be a mom then, and so she had made an adoption plan for April.

"We thought we'd put it into perspective," Faith said. "We were aware of the danger of children mistrusting love if they construed that they were 'given up because they were loved.' We thought we'd given her an accurate picture. And we talked about the new baby, how wonderful were both adoption and birth, how we loved our two children."

Faith continued, "I knew my husband and I had some more explaining to do, however, when I heard April's assertion once her friends had finished ooh-ing and ahh-ing over her baby brother. 'Soon we'll take him to our adoption agency,' she said. 'We love him, and so we're going to take him there to be adopted.'"

❖

Chadd: age seven

"Well, I just want to know who I look like. Everybody says Matt looks just like Daddy. But who do I look like? Can't I see a picture?" seven-year-old Chadd had asked.

"Of course I began to worry," Chadd's mother Laura explained, "but then my friends say I worry too much about our kids! Anyway, I was concerned that Chadd was feeling especially left out since Matt, our biological son, did in fact look like a clone of his father, Jon.

"A lucky thing happened when we were at our agency one day. We had just stopped by to pick up materials for a meeting we were hosting at our house, and the boys were with us. Jon picked up an album of hundreds of children the agency had placed in homes over the years. Chadd looked over his dad's shoulder as they leafed slowly through the album. All he kept saying was: 'Wow, all those kids!' but I could almost read his thoughts: 'All those kids don't really know who they look like either. I'm not alone.'"

❖

Jason: age seven

Helen and Ray had been getting little hints of late that their son, who was born into their family sixteen months after they had adopted his big sister, was beginning to feel that adoption was the preferable method of joining a family.

"Which do you think is neater?" Ray asked him, "to be born into a family or adopted into a family?"

"To be adopted into a family," Jason said with confidence. After all, he had heard so many conversations about adoption and relatively few about the process of birth.

"Guess what," Helen interrupted. "We didn't care where a baby came from. Daddy and I wanted so much to have a baby in our family that we didn't care if it dropped out of the sky. And here we were, lucky enough to get you, the most terrific boy that any family could ever want. So it doesn't matter, born or adopted, we have a wonderful son that we love with all our hearts."

"Our son had nothing more to say," Helen reports, "and we feel we had closed the conversation down with our hasty assertions. While we would eventually have wanted to state our feelings, we wish we had asked more questions and allowed him to state *his* feelings more thoroughly first."

❖

Kris: age seven

"Our daughter was about seven or eight when she said something amazingly compassionate about her little sister," Cori said. "Kris was already five when we adopted Kit, and so she understood the difference in their arrivals into our family.

"Would you believe, one day Kris said, 'Mom, I don't want to hurt your feelings, but I kind of wish I could have grown in the same woman's tummy that Kit grew in so she wouldn't feel different.' Of course I assured her that we loved them both and that they were both absolutely a part of our family, but that it was very thoughtful of her to be concerned about her sister's feelings."

❖

Peter: age seven

"But why did she do that? Why did she give her baby to us? Mommy, ... you wouldn't give me away, would you?"

"Never, never, never, Peter. And it must have been terribly hard for her to decide on adoption for your beautiful new baby sister. Daddy and I only met her that one time at the agency, you know, but she said it was the hardest choice she'd ever made.   I'll bet it's the hardest thing she'll ever do in her whole life. Can you think of why she might have made such a hard choice?" Lydia asked.

"Was she too young to be a mom? That's what dad said."

"She said she didn't think she was ready to be a mom like she'd want to be for her baby. And she thought we'd be the family she'd like her baby to grow up in and be a part of. She felt she was doing what was best for her baby and for herself."

"But some moms are young," Peter countered.

"Yes, and they might feel they are ready to be moms. What's best for one person isn't always best for another."

Peter had been shopping around for answers, having asked his father some of the same questions earlier that day. Lydia and Mark felt fortunate that Peter was asking, analyzing, and asking again. Their new daughter would have questions when she was older, but their son, who had been born into their family, had questions now, especially since he was already seven years old.

Lydia and Mark had read all the books on adoption that they could get their hands on before their baby arrived, but not many had addressed the questions of the older biological sibling. However, just as with other issues, they knew to listen carefully to the question, answer truthfully, and answer only what was asked. Since Peter kept coming back for more, the approach seemed right.

"Mom, can I hold the baby again?"

Combination Families

Kristie: age eight

It does happen once in a while. The Crandals adopted Kristie and then the twins—yes, twins—were born 15 months later.

"Kristie had been so young that she didn't really understand the pregnancy or that her arrival in the family had been via another method," Carrie Crandal commented, "and so we explained as the children grew." The three got along famously most of the time, and the Crandals were comfortable that all their children understood the processes of adoption and birth, and that they all felt a part of the family.

Kristie was eight before a feeling surfaced, and of course at eight, children want to be just like everyone else. She evidently tried to cover her feelings just a bit by making a joke, but the joke was not difficult to interpret.

"Was the reason I didn't grow in you because the twins were in there taking up my space?"

❖

Alex: age eight

Alex, who was eight years old and who had been born into the Danielson family, was old enough to ponder the complexities of the adoption of his tiny new brother. His mother Sally had answered or commented on some of his musings, but if she wasn't sure how to answer, she would simply listen and wonder along with Alex.

115

"What about the dad? What did the dad say about the adoption?" Alex asked at one point.

"Daddy and I weren't told too much about him, Alex, but we do know that he and the birthmother made the decision about adoption together."

And later ... "Mom, how could a mommy who isn't ready to be a mommy have a baby?"

Sally took a deep breath and plunged in. "Well, Alex, sometimes teenagers get into intimate relationships that they really aren't ready for. They had sex and had a baby before they were ready to make a commitment to each other. And so then they had a hard decision to make. They really didn't want to get married, and so the birthmother had to decide if she was ready to be a parent all by herself—or it could have been the birthfather all by himself—or if they wanted to make an adoption plan for their baby. Obviously they decided that for the baby and for themselves, adoption was the best choice."

A silence followed.

"But, come on, you still haven't told me much about your first day of school. Is Ben in your room again this year?"

"Yeah. But, mom, it's awful. It was *my* first day of school, and all the teachers just asked about the baby."

"Oh, ouch," Sally grimaced along with Alex. "Come here, cowboy, this mom needs a hug."

❖

Jason: age nine

"It's the family reunions that bother me," Barbara said. "Jason at nine was quite concerned about, are you ready, the fact that he was not a biological part of our family but looked so much like all of us anyway. He actually looks more like his dad than Daniel, who was born to us, does! I knew everyone would come in the door at Thanksgiving and, since we hadn't seen many of them for quite a while, they were going to say, 'Oh, Jason, you look so much like your dad. Doesn't he look just like his dad?' which would make Jason very uncomfortable at this point. So, I decided to try to intervene, and I asked each family as we were making plans earlier by phone to please not say that. I told them that Jason was a bit touchy about the subject just now.

"I don't know if that was wise or not. It pretty much worked, but I know that's not handling the issue. On the other hand, we just didn't feel this was the right time to deal with that particular issue."

"I was dreading our family reunion last summer for the same reason," Karen said. "It's a huge family of towheads, including our biological daughter. And along comes Mark with his darker brown hair and more olive skin. I'm not sure if it bothers him or if it just bothers me worrying about whether it bothers him!

"I realized *after* the reunion what I could have said to help Mark, and I'm going to try it before the next get-together. With Mark, I can diffuse things by bringing them up beforehand, and I wish I'd said, on our way out to the lake, 'Well, here we go again where everybody looks alike, hmm?' I'm not sure where that opener would have led or if it would have led anywhere. I think just saying it would have been helpful. We do use a lot of humor in our family, and if appropriate, I might have added, 'Well, let them eat their hearts out when they get their sunburns and you get your great tan.'"

Timmy: age nine

"But who is her real mother? You're not her real brother, are you, Timmy?" asked his friend Jerry.

"Mom says I'm her real brother. Mom, that's right, isn't it?" Timmy looked questioningly at Joyce as she was changing the baby who had arrived at their house amid fanfare on the part of the neighborhood just days earlier.

Joyce said it again, and knew it wouldn't be the last time. "Oh, yes, we're her family—forever. Whoever raises you, who you live with, is your family. Timmy's got a sister, all right.

"And just wait until she's big enough to keep up with you boys. She looks like she'll be able to take care of herself, doesn't she. Look at that fist. She's going to grasp a tennis racket in no time!"

The boys gazed admiringly at the adorable face with the turned up nose. Joyce had tried to answer the boys' questions but then to keep them from dwelling only on the fact that Abby had entered their family through adoption. That was one facet of Abby, but there were many more.

❖

Troy and Leslie: ages nine and eleven

The Johnsons had two biological children, Leslie eleven and Troy nine, and so, since they were that old, the adoption of an infant sibling had been a family adventure. All four of the Johnsons had anxiously awaited "the call" from the agency. The excitement had been unanimous when it finally came. "A sister. A baby sister!" Leslie beamed.

When the social worker from the agency arrived during that first week for a visit, she spoke with Leslie and Troy, with whom she'd built a familiar relationship during the preceding months.

"*Now* would you rather have a dog?" she teased Troy, reminding him of the time he'd said that to her in jest as his mother winced.

"Naw, she's okay," he rejoined. "You could have gotten a boy, though. Now they'll gang up on me!"

Leslie was more serious. "Kids are asking so much stuff about her. Everybody's nice, but I wonder if she'll get teased sometime because she'd adopted. If she does, how do we help her?"

The social worker paused for a time. "Leslie, the fact that you even asked tells me that you'll do fine."

❖

Stuart: age nine

Since Deirdre serves on fundraising committees for their agency, there always seemed to be lots of "adoption talk" in their house. Mail and newsletters come regularly with "adoption" headlines and agency logos. Small wonder, then, that their son, Stuart, who was born into the Drake family two years after they adopted his sister, began to tell friends that he, too, had been adopted.

"I'm aware that most, or at least many, children have adoption fantasies at his age," Deirdre said. "However, a few conversations with Stuart left my husband and me with the definite feeling that it was more than fantasy, that it fit more into the category of a wish. Adoption must be pretty important, after all, if it rated all those meetings with dessert and the best china.

"The perfect solution finally occurred to me. I had had recent conversations with several of the neighborhood mothers about safety rules since our children were getting to the ages where they could go to the park with a friend, could ride their bikes on certain streets, et cetera.

"I asked these mothers if they would care to meet regularly to discuss these issues, to keep ahead of our concerns. They were as eager to do that as I was.

"And so for the past three years, eight of us have met one morning a month at my house. We tell our children our collective decisions: We lock up their bikes for a week with our own combination locks if they ride without helmets, for instance.

"The rewards have been multiple. No child so much as argued about a bike helmet thereafter! We parents feel we're not alone. My daughter actually suggested once that I 'ask the moms' about our disagreement concerning how late she and her friends could stay up at her sleep-over birthday party. The children realize their actions may be discussed at our next 'Moms' Meeting.' We may well have created in our neighborhood that ingredient of accountability which we wistfully read about in articles recalling life as it used to be in Small Town, USA.

"As far as my son is concerned, I think this focus has helped him see that it's quite fine to be born into a family, too! Once he asked me, 'What do you do at your meetings for three hours? That seems like a long time to talk.'

"I took that opportunity to answer, 'Oh, we talk about everything! Dancing lessons and allowances and braces. And sometimes we talk about how neat it was when you were born, and how much fun it is to do things now that you can handle so much.'

"I'm positive Stuart held his breath for a brief time when I said 'We talk about how neat it was when you were born.' I might have imagined it, but I could almost feel him basking in that ray of sunlight.

"He never misses making some small observation about each meeting. Just a little comment as he eyes the china when I lay it out on the dining room table the night before."

"Moms' Meeting tomorrow?"

❖

Chapter Six

Birthparents

The preschool child is not self-centered: He is simply totally egocentric! It is generally beyond his capabilities, intellectually, to put himself into another's position and see that person's point of view.

While the preschool child who was adopted may be told about his birthparents and be able to repeat facts, a skill at which he can be very adept, it is the school-aged child who actually begins to "understand past events when they are closely associated with the present." Will the school-aged child who was adopted begin suddenly to see the stories about his "coming home" in a new light, begin to ask with real understanding more about the "before"?

While the relationship between the adolescent and his parents is often ambivalent, adults outside the family are frequently viewed by the young person in one of many ways. They may be treated as extensions of parents (All adults are alike); they may be treated as so different and dense that they cannot be communicated with (All adults are "out of it"); or they may be treated as opposites of parents, idealized (Adolescent gets crush on teacher). Might the adolescent who was adopted similarly categorize the adult world, and, in addition, idealize or think negatively about unknown birthparents?

Interest in birthparents during adolescence, even intense interest, may or may not lead to discussion of the subject, however. The need of the adolescent to be separate and independent from his parents as well as feelings of loyalty to his family, intermittently intense in many adolescents, may keep him from asking questions and thereby showing interest in his birthparents at this stage.

Nearly all the dialogues in this chapter, perhaps predictably, take place between parents and their children of school age.

❖

Jenny: age five

Janet was on the phone longer than she'd expected to be. When she came back into the family room, the children's program was over and her five-year-old daughter was engrossed in a documentary about babies born with drug addictions. With seemingly perfect understanding and clarity, Jenny said, "The mother who had me in her tummy didn't take drugs because she knew you wanted me to be healthy."

❖

Kevin: age six

"I'm losing sleep over the question my six-year-old son Kevin has not asked me yet, but one I'm sure he will ask sooner or later," Kaye began. "It will be the question most children who were adopted ask. It will be, 'Why did my birthmother have me be adopted?'

Birthparents

"While I know the standard answers to the standard situations, Kevin's background is complicated. I can't respond that his birthmother felt she was too young to be a parent at that time. She was a parent already and was raising an older sibling. Another level of complexity was added when I learned recently that she had subsequently given birth to a third child whom she chose to parent.

"How can I help my son come to terms with this information? First of all, unless he asks it all at once, I think I will answer only his immediate question. I will tell him truthfully in answer to his first question that the woman who gave birth to him didn't feel she could take care of a new baby at that point in her life.

"I am thankful that Kevin is a resiliant child, and I think and hope, since he feels such a part of our family, that he will handle the additional information when he is ready to ask the questions.

"My answer will have to include the truthful statement that I don't know why she chose adoption for him, but that I am certain it did not reflect on him but rather on her circumstances at the time. I will ask him to speculate with me about possible reasons. I will assure him that I am positive it was a difficult decision for her and that the reasons were undoubtedly weighty.

"Will this circumstance make Kevin's acceptance of his adoption more difficult for him than it is for most children? Maybe. But each child comes to terms with his life's story in his own way, and I will trust that my son will find his way. This is a very poetic answer, but I think it's the only one there is."

❖

Birthparents

Drew: age six

"Wouldn't it have been neat," Drew began, looking up at his mother, "wouldn't it have been neat if I'd been twins? Then you could have had one of me, and my birthmother could have had one of me—and then she'd get to see what a neat kid I am!"

❖

Lara: age seven

"Mom," Elizabeth's daughter Lara said, out of the blue. "Can I see the woman who birthed me?"

"Well, honey," Elizabeth responded, giving herself a moment to collect her thoughts, "you've just asked a very complicated question. Daddy and I never saw her, you know. She wasn't at the agency when we first saw you."

"Oh, I know, but can't I just see her?"

"Well, first of all, you can't when you're a child."

"Oh, then when I'm an adult?" Lara asked with hope in her voice.

"Well, it's still more complicated than that. When you are an adult, you will have a choice to make. You can choose to try to locate her, or you can choose not to. If you decide not to, that's okay. If you decide to try, that's okay, too. And if you decide to try, Daddy and I will help you if you would like us to."

Birthparents

"Oh, I'll want to. I'll want to."

"There is one thing, though," Elizabeth felt obligated to add. "She would have to want this, too."

That took a few minutes to sink in. But Elizabeth felt good that she had told her daughter the whole truth. And she felt her daughter did, too.

❖

Meredith: age seven

Meredith had been at Karen's birthday party all afternoon. The girls were best of friends and lived just houses apart, and so they had gotten to know each other's families well. "Perhaps this familiarity was what made Meredith comfortable about sharing birthfamily fantasies with the entire party of seven-year-olds!" thought her mother, Ruth.

Karen's parents had shown up at Ruth's door not long after the party ended. It seems Meredith had been telling the girls that she had seven brothers when in fact she has one!

"At first we assumed she was doing a little fanciful fabricating," they said. "And then we realized she might have been talking about other children her birthmother might have had, and so we left it alone. Does Meredith actually know if her birthmother had other children?"

Ruth appreciated the way her neighbors had worded their question. They were obviously very curious, but they had simply asked if Meredith knew the facts so that they could respond appropriately in the future. They hadn't asked what those facts were.

"No," Ruth responded. "This has never come up, and as a matter of fact, we don't even know. Thanks for just letting her have her little fantasy."

❖

Phillip: age eight

Phillip was eight when it occurred to him that, in addition to birthparents, there might be other people out there to whom he was biologically related. Certainly his birthparents' parents, but perhaps his birthparents had brothers and sisters as well.

"I did have that information," Lil said, "and I decided this was the right time to share it with Phillip. I was able to tell him that his birthfather, in fact, had come from a very large family comprised of nine children."

"*All* those people out there ..." was Phillip's first reaction.

He reflected in silence for a time. And then a glimmer appeared in his eye. "Why, I could just pop in on my grandfather and say, 'Here I am!'"

"I had to help him face the reality of the situation, and so I gently interjected the fact that this was a two-way street, and that everyone had to be comfortable with such a scenario," Lil continued. "But I assured him that, as we had discussed in the past, he might in fact choose to attempt to locate his birthparents when he became an adult. Within the last few minutes, that consideration had multiplied by nine for Phillip!"

Birthparents

Andrew: age eight

"Mom, come quick. A baby squirrel has fallen out of its nest," Andrew shouted. "Hurry!"

Renee ran outside with Andrew where they discovered not one, but two, baby squirrels under the tree. They were so tiny that their eyes were still closed. They kept trying to get up but would fall immediately. Their slow but steady progress was widening the gap between them. Soon they wouldn't even have each other.

Andrew was a born animal lover, and even at age eight he had refrained from touching the baby squirrels. But since it was evident that they would not be rescued by the mother squirrel, Andrew and Renee quickly made a soft nest in a box for the tiny animals.

"Mom, we have to feed them," Andrew said soberly. "What can they eat when they're so tiny?"

"Surely their mother was still nursing them," Renee said, aware of Andrew's intense concern. "You warm some milk in the microwave and I'll find a tiny eyedropper."

It was hard to tell if the squirrels were getting any nourishment or not from Andrew's efforts. The milk ran out of their mouths. "Mom," Andrew said, this time sounding a bit desperate, "I don't know if I'm old enough to take care of the baby squirrels."

The phone rang, and Andrew's father Blake was on the line. Renee quickly explained the situation to him, telling him of Andrew's concern about whether he was old enough to assume the care of these little charges.

Blake got the message. "This is incredible. He's thinking of his birthmother. It's probably really important that we help him now, but that we don't just take the situation out of his hands. Why don't you call Kisha. I know she used to volunteer for the Humane Society. She might know where we can get help or advice."

Fortunately, Kisha knew. There happened to be a "Squirrel Lady," as everyone affectionately called her, who would take injured or orphaned squirrels, or just give advice when needed. Renee phoned her, explained their dilemma, and Squirrel Lady asked to talk to Andrew.

She explained to Andrew that, since the squirrels were so tiny, it would probably be very difficult to keep them healthy. But she said she would be glad to help Andrew try. She said he sounded like a very responsible and caring boy. But she said if it seemed like it would be too hard a job for Andrew, and she realized he was quite young, she would be glad to take care of the babies herself since she had helped many baby squirrels in the past.

Renee saw that Andrew needed some time to think and talk, and so she asked Squirrel Lady if they could call her back.

"You have a choice, dear," Renee said gently. "And you know I'm here to help if you need me. But Daddy and I think you should decide."

It didn't take Andrew long to decide. He would gladly have put in the effort, but he could see how helpless the newborn animals were. And that made him feel pretty helpless at age eight. "Mom, I'm going to call Squirrel Lady. I know she can take care of them, and I'd feel so bad if they died."

Birthparents

"Let's get in the car so that we can get them to her quickly," Renee said. "And remember, Andrew, you've done something very wonderful for the squirrels by saving them and bringing them to Squirrel Lady."

Andrew told his father all about Squirrel Lady that evening. Later, as Blake and Renee talked privately, they discussed the depth of Andrew's feelings that were so evident, and, in fact, the depth of their own feelings over the incident.

"Let's wait a while," Blake said, "but sometime when it comes up naturally, let's help Andrew consider the similarities of his feelings to-day and what must have been his birthmother's feelings. I'm sure he knows it on some level, and I think it will be good for him to put it into words."

❖

Erin: age nine

"Mom," Priscilla's preteen daughter Erin mused, "do you think now my birthmother would want to keep me? Do you think she'd let me be adopted if I were born to her now? She'd be 25, wouldn't she?"

"Something tells me she'd be able to be a mother now, honey, and that she'd be delighted to be. She was just so young when you were born..." Priscilla responded.

"I know. She was a kid herself. I'd like to talk to her."

"That would be nice, wouldn't it."

Birthparents

Laura: age nine

"I wrote my best composition ever today," fourth-grader Laura announced as she jumped into the car after school. "Mrs. Davenport gave us the title 'The Most Important Person In My Life,' and we had to write about that."

"That sounds interesting," her mother Mary responded. "Do I get to hear it?"

"Sure," said Laura enthusiastically.

Here it is below, letter perfect, and copied with Laura's permission.

The Most Important Person

The most important person in my life is my birthmother because if it hadn't been for her I wouldn't be here writing this.

I don't remember her but maybe she remembers me from when I was born.

I think that when I grow up I will go to the adoption center and ask if someone could help me find my birthmother if she is still alive and well.

And when I find her I will invite her over for dinner. And ask a lot of questions about when I was born. And what I looked like when I was born. And what I looked like and things that a child that was adopted would ask.

"Yes, Laura," her mother responded. "It was a wonderful composition. I'm so proud of you. Thanks for sharing your best composition yet."

Birthparents

Deborah: age eleven

"Mom," eleven-year-old Deborah began, "when can I find out stuff about my birthmother?"

Through previous discussions, Deborah had come to realize that the possibility of searching for the woman who gave birth to her was a decision she would make as an adult. But learning facts about her was another question and one her mother Janet wasn't sure about either.

"I guess I don't really know, honey. But we can find out. How about if we call the agency and ask them what you are allowed to learn and when," Janet ventured.

Deborah was delighted at this prospect and made sure her mom placed the call quickly.

"Yes, of course we would be happy to talk with Deborah," the caseworker said. "Perhaps you and your husband would like to stop in first to look through materials, see which ones you already have so that I can get a packet ready for Deborah, and we could discuss the approach you have taken so that I can complement it."

Later at the agency, as Janet and her husband Richard looked through the files containing information (but no names or addresses), the caseworker offered that they could take home to Deborah at that time anything they thought would be of interest to her. "She can look through it before I meet with her and then she may have questions."

"I suggest," she continued, "that you take any information pertaining to her own babyhood. Often this is what an eleven-year-old is most interested in, even if her actual questions are about her birthmother."

"One other suggestion. Though this hasn't always been our approach, we now think it wise for you to give this information privately to your daughter, but with the understanding that she will share it with her brother when, not if, she is ready."

"Oh, and by the way, don't be concerned if Deborah decides at the last moment that she doesn't want to come to see me after all. It often happens. Just assure her we'll always be here and she can come later if she chooses. Janet's unspoken thought was, "You just don't know my daughter. She'll be here!"

Deborah was positively thrilled with the papers her parents gave her that evening. She clutched her precious packet as she went to bed, and they knew she'd read and reread far into the night. She checked and rechecked that date when she would actually go to the agency with her dad and mother. She marked the date on her calendar. It was a red-letter day in her mind.

Something touching and gratifying occurred the next evening. Janet and Richard had gone out for a quick errand, leaving the children at home alone. When they returned, Deborah and her nine-year-old brother were sprawled on the floor pouring over "her papers." Both were ooh-ing and ahh-ing, both enthralled, her brother as delighted for Deborah as she was for herself. It was a picture-perfect sharing.

But it was "the meeting," scheduled for the following Thursday, that most excited Deborah. Daily she would check with her mother. "The meeting is still set for next Thursday, isn't it?"

Thursday finally arrived. When Deborah came home from school that afternoon, Janet suddenly realized there was some uneasiness in the air. Deborah wasn't sure what to wear. Would she have to ask questions, or could her dad and mom? Janet assured her they would help in any way she'd like them to.

Deborah, a glum Deborah, and her mother got into the car. They were to meet Richard at the agency. It was only a ten-minute ride, an unhappy ten minutes. Suddenly Deborah burst forth with the fact that she didn't want to go. Today. Or ever. Moreover, the agency was a stupid old place, and she never ever wanted to go in there.

Such were her fears.

How grateful Janet was that she'd been warned of this possibility. She was able to calmly and gently assure Deborah that it was perfectly fine, that she didn't have to go. That she could go at some other time if she'd like. That she need never go if she so chose.

But they did need to stop at the agency now. They needed to tell the caseworker that they wouldn't be coming today. Daddy would be wondering where they were. Janet asked Deborah if she would come in with her, assuring Deborah that no one would be upset about the cancellation of their appointment.

Janet was hoping, of course, that Deborah would walk inside with her just so that she could see there was nothing to fear, so that she would feel comfortable returning at a later date if she desired.

But her strong-willed daughter had her mind made up. No, she would not go in. She would wait in the car. Period.

The caseworker saved the day. Rather against Janet's better judgment, she insisted on coming out to the car to say hello to Deborah. Janet's concern was that Deborah, in her present state of mind, might be less than polite. She was. But the experienced caseworker took it in stride, assured Deborah that all was well and that she had just wanted to meet Deborah and assure her that she could come back at any time if she chose. After flashing Janet another this-happens-all-the-time smile, the caseworker went back into the building that Janet hoped seemed friendly to her daughter.

To date, nearly a year later, Deborah has not asked for more information. She does initiate a "birthmother conversation" once or twice a month. Janet sees her "papers" stacked in different places in her room, and assumes that means Deborah reads them on occasion.

Will Deborah want to know more some day? "Knowing my daughter," answers Janet, " I would think she will. But, then, I said that once before, didn't I?"

❖

Garrick, Morgan, and Celeste: ages ten, eight, and six

"I've wondered how much a part personality plays in how children deal with the stories of their adoption," Emily said.

"Our older child is as matter-of-fact as they come. He is practical in all aspects of his life. I've heard Garrick answer a friend's query about his birthmother by saying, 'She couldn't raise me. She was too young.' End of conversation.

"While the situation for the birthmother of our daughter was in fact similar, Morgan insists on another version. Even though we correct her, she has volunteered a number of times that her birthmother is dead. 'She was poor and she died,' our fantasy-oriented daughter declares.

Birthparents

We may need to talk soon about the possibility that this is how it feels to Morgan. I'm not very concerned at this point, however, because creating stories does fit with her personality. A little embellishment is her style.

"Which reminds me of a friend whose child came up with a whopper," Emily continued.

"My birthmother tried to kill me with a knife," Celeste had explained to classmates. One of the children had repeated the story to her mother, who had called Celeste's parents, friends of hers.

When her parents asked Celeste about the story she had told her classmates, Celeste readily and rather proudly admitted what she had said. Her parents pursued the matter, gently insisting, "You know why your birthmother really decided on adoption, Celeste. Why did you tell your friends otherwise?"

"Well," Celeste countered, "that story is really boring."

❖

Adult to adult

"If it ever came to that," Marie's close and perceptive friend asked, "how would you feel about meeting your daughter's birthmother?"

"My daughter is only eight," Marie stalled, "and so I haven't thought much about it yet.

"But if the possibility were to present itself right now—let me see. I'm not threatened by the idea. I know my daughter loves me, and I know you can love more than one person.

Birthparents

"At the moment, the silliest thing occurs to me. I was 36 when Gretchen came to us. Her birthmother was less than half my age. What a vain thing to admit, but what comes to mind is how young and beautiful she will be!

"I know this is perfectly ridiculous, that people aren't loved or not loved because of appearance. But you asked for my feelings. A tinge of jealousy, with, I suppose, a touch of fear behind it. If I'm honest, those are my feelings right now."

❖

Adult to adult

The Gray's children were still very small, but Diana and Jeff were attending a seminar on adoption to ready themselves for the eventual discussions they would have with their children. A class participant was explaining to the group how she had dealt with her seven-year-old daughter's repeated comments and queries about her birthmother.

It was the constant comments that had begun to irritate this mother. "I'll bet my birthmother is pretty ... I wonder if my birthmother is a good dancer like I am ... I wonder if my birthmother has a prettier house than we have ... I know my birthmother loves me very, very much ... I wish I could see my birthmother."

The mother had been patiently commiserating with her daughter's every utterance until one day she evidently reached her limit.

"Remember, she *did* give you away," she said to her daughter.

"We all can and do make mistakes," said Diana as she recounted the incident to a friend. "That's true of any subject or any exchange we have with our children. I heard a speaker not long ago say that when we make a mess, we can broach the subject later when the intensity is gone. If in fact the exchange had bothered our child, conversation about it can ameliorate the difficulty. If the child had not been sensitive to what had happened, he will shrug it off and we can know we needn't pursue the concern. If it was an egregious error on the parent's part, an explanation of why he or she responded so might be in order. In other words, it was not this mom's response that bothered me as I look back on it. It was her attitude toward her response."

This well-meaning, gentle mother had triumphantly reported to the group, "It's been two years, and Melissa has never brought it up again. That was exactly what she needed to hear."

"The mother had interpreted the welcomed silence as resolution to her daughter's continual questioning," Diana continued, "questioning that may, at second glance, have been signaling a confusion about something beyond the overt comments, or perhaps just evidence of the fact that concerns about adoption are rarely 'settled' but return, often cyclically, and signal a new developmental phase of the child and his depth of understanding about adoption.

"I'm not sure why no one in the group questioned this exchange. My daughter was a toddler at the time and I was just at the beginning stages of building my repertory of responses to future questions, and so, while the mother's words had shocked me, it didn't occur to me to question the technique. This situation does speak favorably for 'gut reactions', however. I knew something was wrong, and this conversation has managed to linger in my mind for the many years that have passed since that meeting.

"My own daughter is now twelve, and we have had countless and poignant and honest conversations regarding her birthmother. Though I'm certainly not trying to say I have made no mistakes, I feel very fortunate that my daughter and I have been able to keep our lines of communication open thus far. I'm afraid that the other mother may have inadvertently closed some of those lines forever."

❖

Adult to adult

"'Musings of a Mom' might be an appropriate title to my thoughts," Carol ventured. "It's been so easy for me all these years, while my daughter was growing up, to talk with her about birthparents. Sometimes months would go by and the issue of adoption never arose, but then Alissa would have another question or comment. I gradually grew to trust our ability to communicate about this subject just as we communicated well about everything else.

"And so now my feelings take me by surprise. My daughter is nearly mature and we do know that her birthmother would like to meet her, if those are Alissa's wishes, too.

"And I'm ... scared. I've always said, 'I know my daughter loves me. Love and caring from another adult can only enhance a young person's life. Alissa's love for me won't change even if she should learn to know her birthmother well and grow to love her, too.'

"But now that the time has come, I find myself asking, 'Or will it change things?'

"We're not talking about an additional aunt, here. Nor are we talking about the extra grandmas and grandpas that come with remarriage. We're talking about the woman who gave birth to my daughter.

"On the other hand, don't things always change? Things changed that first day I dropped my daughter off at nursery school, placing her in someone else's hands. It was never quite the same again. In the years that followed, the voice of absolute authority became 'teacher's.' 'But my *teacher* said...' was always the last word on a subject.

"The first best friend and the constant sleep-overs changed things. My daughter learned that our family's ways were not the only ways. Not to mention sleep-over camp. She always returned a different person— there's no other way to say it.

"When she became a favorite neighborhood babysitter, I realized the change. Suddenly she was the responsible one in someone else's home. She was in charge at those times. She handled things, and she *could* handle things very well. And did that change our relationship? Yes, it did. She became more independent, but she also became more under- standing. I still smile at our first conversation about how trying little children can be when they won't obey.

"And let's not forget the first boyfriend. Suddenly there was in my daughter's smile a gentleness I'd never seen before, a realization of her own womanhood. And there passed between us the unspoken knowl- edge that she was no longer a little girl. We had become equals in some essential way.

"Now the question is, did these leaps in my daughter's maturing process diminish our relationship in any way? Of course the answer is no. But each one did indeed change it.

"Here is probably the crux of my fear. This experience is unknown to most of my friends and relatives with whom I can share joys or concerns involving these other milestones. Every mom has had the nursery school experience, the best friend experience, the babysitting experience.

"But even though I have a large group of friends who are adoptive mothers, I actually don't know a single one who has been through the 'meeting the birthmother' experience with her child. Although I know many second-hand stories and I've read many books, it's a relative unknown, and I feel alone out there, all the more so since I know experiences can differ widely.

"One keeps seeing the blissful and the horrendous sensationalized on television. Certainly this has added to my apprehension, although we have reason to believe that in our daughter's case, everything would be fine.

"What gives me courage, once all this has been said, is to realize that all the changes thus far have enhanced my daughter as a person and have enhanced our mother-daughter relationship. I will simply trust that this one will, too."

❖

Chapter Seven

Friends

Preschool friends of a child who was adopted may occasionally show interest in his adoption. Typically, however, it is the adopted child himself who wants to explain the phenomenon to his young friends, who may or may not show much enthusiasm for his revelations at this point.

Friends of the school-aged child, on the other hand, will often show intense interest in adoption and ask many questions, for this is the time of great curiousity for all children about all topics, and any differences are subject to review.

Children of school age, adopted or born to their families, also often have "adoption fantasies" at this age, thinking they themselves were really born to some royal family but are being raised in this rather pedestrian home. These fantasies, on the part of children who were in fact born to their families, may confuse them as they hear about the actual adoptions of friends.

Companions are important to school-aged children, and it is often a time of the "best friend." Friendships are frequently shifting and short-lived, however, and today's favorite may be teased tomorrow. Close cooperation between parents and teachers is essential at this time if a child is being teased about his adoption.

The teacher of the six-year-old realizes the tendencies of her charges. She understands the frequent friendship shifts, and she knows that the

extreme behavior—teasing, bossing, tattling, complaining—are a part
of the stage, but they are not to be excessively tolerated.

The friends of the adolescent who was adopted, themselves now aware
of various situations that can lead to the placement of a child for adoption and of many of the legalities involved, often ask him about his
particular background. Perhaps because there have been so many television shows dedicated to the subject, young people sometimes ask questions that are highly inappropriate: "How much did your parents pay
for you?" being a common query, especially of children adopted
transracially and whose adoptions are therefore evident.

In addition, TV talk-show talk often becomes hostile as groups of people
involved with adoption conflict, and therefore the understanding of adoption by adolescents can be badly skewed. Discussing with the adolescent who was adopted how and when and if intrusive questions from
friends should be answered can be helpful even if the adolescent shrugs
and says, "It doesn't bother me."

Vignettes offered for this chapter were almost exclusively those that
involved the friends of school-aged children. Some stories placed in
other chapters, however, illustrate adolescents' interest in the subject.

❖

Josh and Brett: ages five and six

Sharon's sister Beth had brought her children to play for the afternoon,
and the women sat on the terrace while the three cousins entertained
themselves at the picnic table not far away.

Friends

"My mom says you weren't born into your family. She said you were adopted. That's not true, is it?" they heard six-year-old Brett ask his five-year-old cousin, Josh.

Josh rose to the occasion. "Of course it's true," he asserted. "And," he added with five-year-old profundity, "if you were born into our family, you would have been adopted, too."

They all turned back to the clay zoo they were creating and Josh muttered, more to himself than anyone, "This is the way it is. That's a coo-coo question."

❖

Ann Marie: age five

The conversation around the sand table had begun spontaneously in nursery school that day. First one child, and then the next, told where he had been born.

"I was born in California."

"I was born in Silver Spring."

"I was born in Children's Hospital in Washington, DC."

Ann Marie, whose parents had adopted her in Colombia, didn't miss a beat.

"I was chosen," was all she said.

❖

Friends

Molly: age six

Margie was glad she was driving the car pool for the three first-grade girls the day it came up. One little girl called to Margie's daughter, "Molly, I heard something weird about you. Megan says you're adopted."

"Yes," Margie quickly interrupted. "That's another way of building a family."

Molly chimed right in with additional information. "Some kids are birthed," she said. "And some kids are birthed and then adopted."

The conversation changed to another subject. "Maybe I'll be lucky enough to be there for the probable follow-up," Margie thought. "But if I'm not, I think Molly can manage."

❖

Max: age seven

Max interrupted his non-stop playing at the company picnic long enough to rush over to his mother and enthusiastically say, "I met this great kid. And guess what—he was adopted, too!"

Shelly had met the boy's parents earlier, and now she wandered over to them and mentioned what a good time their boys were having. They had noticed, too, and they all made plans then and there to picnic together the next weekend.

Shelly was elated. A new friend is a wonderful gift, and this boy was adopted as well. If the children had so readily shared this fact with each

146

other, they might well have other adoption conversations in the future. There was obviously no certainty that the relationship would continue as it had begun, but it was definitely worth an attempt to foster such a friendship.

❖

Duncan: age seven

Pat was driving car pool that day, and another one of those in-the-car conversations about adoption took place. Pat's ears perked up when she heard Duncan, one of the three second-grade boys, announce, "I'm going to adopt a kid when I grow up."

"Why would you want to do that?" another boy questioned. "It might turn out to be a rotten kid like the one that was in the movie *Problem Child*."

❖

Gillian: age seven

"Sally and Jessica were asking me stuff about my birthmother today," Gillian told her mother in what Carmen interpreted to be a defensive voice. "They wanted to know how old she was when she birthed me."

"Honey," Carmen answered, "you know Daddy and I want you to feel free to tell anyone you would like to about your adoption. Some people you will want to tell just the fact that you were adopted. Others you'll want to tell a little more. Some very good friends you might want to tell many of the details about it.

"But there's one thing I guess we haven't talked about. And that is— some people you don't have to tell *anything* about your adoption. And if you don't feel like it, then it's none of their business, and you don't have to say a word. You don't insist on their telling you the details of how they got here, and they don't have to ask you details unless you want to share. You can feel free to just change the subject."

"Oh," Gillian responded, sounding relieved.

❖

Amy: age seven

The director of the school had seen Amy looking uncharacteristically crestfallen and had sauntered over to the swings during recess.

"Hi," she said, "what's happening here?"

"Well," said Amy, "Jennie and April say my mom and dad aren't my real mom and dad because I'm adopted."

"Oh, goodness," the director replied with a sentence that will forever endear her to Amy's parents, "of course Amy's mom and dad are her real mom and dad. Whoever raises you are your real mom and dad. Now, let's see who can swing the highest."

❖

Friends

Allie: age seven

"I hadn't intended, at her tender age of seven, to tell my daughter the exact age at which her birthmother had given birth to her—only that she had been so young that she did not feel she could parent a child, any child, at her age," Clarissa said.

But Allie had somehow pulled it out of her mother, and the consequence was that she was broadcasting the fact near and far, to casual friends and Brownie troop alike.

"I knew I needed to intervene, and once when we were alone and cozy, I brought up the subject," Clarissa continued.

"Sweetheart, you know you can tell anyone you choose about your adoption, but there's one thing you might want to think about. Some details are details you might want to tell everyone, and then some details you might want to save—just for yourself and your family and maybe for some of your closest friends."

"Mom," Allie retorted, knowing instantly to what Clarissa was referring, "you can't rule my life."

"You're absolutely right, honey. But I need to say this. A mom—whether she's an adoptive mom or a birthmom—who sees her little girl doing something that the little girl might be sorry for later, is going to tell her little girl. And then, of course, the little girl has to choose. All I'm asking you to do right now is to listen and to think about it."

A silence. And then a wee voice: "I'm listening."

❖

149

Friends

Kari: age seven

"Mom," second-grader Kari said, displaying a rather puzzled demeanor as she jumped into the car at carpool time, "Jill and Suzie say that I'm not adopted."

"Goodness," her mother Joanne responded, "I wonder why they'd say something like that?"

A long pause. "Well, I think they're jealous."

"Hmmm, that really could be. Another thing occurs to me. It's something that happens when children are about seven, Kari. Many kids, for some reason, think they were adopted. Jill and Suzie may have thought they were adopted, and then someone told them they weren't, and so they might think you weren't either."

"Oh."

Joanne discussed the incident later with her friend, Adrienne, also an adoptive mother. "It brings to mind the debate about whether adoptive parents should prepare their children for teasing that may come their way because they were adopted. At first glance, preparation seems wise. We prepare our children for life. We enable our children to protect themselves by explaining to them and warning them about drugs, early sex, talking to strangers. But do the analogies hold when it comes to teasing?

"At the risk of trivializing adoption, looking at what happens if we 'prepare' our children for other potential teasing may be instructive.

"Your child has just gotten glasses, the greatest pair of designer frames in the shop. He loves them. He's proud of them. He can't wait to show them to everyone."

But you say, "Now, Johnny, kids may call you four-eyes. They may call you a sissy, but you pay no mind. You know they are wrong and are wrong to tease."

"Suddenly Johnny's shoulders have drooped, and the glasses he was so proud of have become a burden," Joanne said.

"I see what you mean," Adrienne interrupted. "Johnny will get teased for sure now."

"Why not handle teasing when and if it happens?" Joanne continued. "True, we may miss some of it if we are not told about something that happened to the child. But that danger must be weighed against the danger of burdening our child with impending doom.

"The subject of teasing can be handled beforehand generically. Talking with our children about what motivates people who tease, the big kid who teases the little kid, the smart—or maybe not-so-smart—kid who teases the not-so-bright, will instruct our child not to tease and it will prepare him, generally, for teasing that might come his way, whether it's about adoption or any other subject.

"If there should be continued teasing, we as parents must step in. At that point, the most effective form of intervention needs to be deter-mined, and action taken. That's true of teasing, whatever the subject.

"If Kari had been 'prepared' for the fact that she might be teased about her adoptive status, she may have received the comments from her friends

151

very differently. She interpreted the motivation for their comments as jealousy. Was it? We'll never know. But if Kari had been expecting to be victimized, she might have felt so. Instead, she felt loved and secure, a security that would not have been enhanced by worry, and her reaction was a positive one."

❖

Andrea: age eight

Andrea and her best friend at school were both adopted as infants. These two formed a bond that was priceless. For an entire year they called each other "sister." Arm in arm they would walk around: "Sister, sister, sister."

One day they announced, "You know, we really could be sisters. We both were adopted."

It was a statement on their part, a caring statement that didn't beg an answer. Both mothers feel fortunate that their daughters are such good friends, and it's a plus that they can comfortably discuss adoption with each other as well.

❖

Sabrina: age eight

Brenda was driving three children, her daughter included, and their teacher on a field trip when she noticed that the conversation in the back seat had turned to the topic of adoption. Two of the girls, it happened, as well as the teacher, had been adopted as infants, a rather unusual scenario.

Suddenly Brenda realized that the third little girl, evidently so as not to feel left out, was protesting that she, too, was adopted. Brenda broke into the conversation amid the 'You were not'... 'I was too' to say, "Sabrina, isn't this something. You and I are the only ones in this car who were born into our families. Isn't that something.

"You know, either way is really neat. It's neat to be adopted into a family and it's neat to be born into a family. The important thing is that we have a family."

And then the conversation went on to typical third-grade-girl talk.

❖

Jodi: age nine

Jodi was just nine, but quite a precocious nine. She was visiting her neighbors the Browns again, an almost daily occurrence.

The Brown family had adopted their two children, and little Lucy had arrived only two weeks earlier. Jodi was very curious about this new-to-her way of having a child enter a family.

"But does she have *real* brothers and sisters? Jackie isn't her *real* brother, is he?" she asked one day, referring to Lucy's four-year-old big brother.

"Oh, yes, Jackie is Lucy's real brother. The family that raises you is your family. Jackie and Lucy and their daddy and I will always be a family," Terri Brown answered.

"But what about her first mommy? What about the mommy where she was born? Why didn't she want to be her mommy?" Jodi continued.

Terri decided that the best way to handle the questions that were, indeed, intrusive, was to give Jodi a brief education about adoption. "Well, sometimes a young woman has a baby at a time when she realizes she just can't be a good parent. And so she decides it would be best for her baby and herself if another family raised the baby. Or sometimes the parents have died, and the child needs a home. There can be many reasons why a child is adopted. And always, the family that adopts a child wants to have a child very much."

Without divulging the details which were for her family alone, Terri helped Jodi understand each facet of adoption as the questions occurred to her. It wasn't a perfect arrangement, Terri knew. Jackie wasn't old enough to be asking those questions himself yet. And yet Jodi was a constant playmate for Jackie, and if not properly educated, Jodi might make comments to Jackie or question him in a way that would confuse him. It seemed better to Terri to answer the questions matter-of-factly and briefly, or Jodi could sense a shroud of secrecy that might only inflame her curiousity and possibly distort her understanding.

By being casual about the topic, Terri sensed that Jodi's questions would eventually stop. And by then, Jodi would be educated but not privy to details that were inappropriate for her to know.

❖

Melissa and Trent: ages eight and ten

"I just can't get over how different Melissa and Trent are," a mother at her children's school remarked to Suzanne as her children, now eight and ten, ran up.

Friends

The woman was not Suzanne's favorite person and had a reputation for being nosy.

"Isn't it amazing?" was all Suzanne decided to say before heading for the car.

It wasn't that Suzanne didn't talk openly about adoption. It was just that there didn't seem to be a reason to share this information with this particular person. And Suzanne never felt obligated along these lines.

But suddenly she was aware of how the exchange may have sounded to her children. Adoption was not something to hide. Was she giving that message to her son and daughter whom she had adopted when they were infants?

Suzanne decided to ask them. "Naa," Trent answered. "She'd just talk about it all the time. You don't need to tell people like her."

❖

Rachael: age eleven

"My daughter was in a class with a particularly viscious group of girls her sixth-grade year," Constance began. "This was not the first time she had come home glum and then burst into tears when the story finally tumbled out. My daughter is very gregarious and wasn't joining any one of the little cliques of girls, which are characteristic of that age.

"The result was that she had no very close friends, either. One group of girls or another would alternately befriend and then taunt Rachael.

155

"This particular day the subject of the teasing concerned me greatly. Rachael, it seems, was branded as stupid because she had been adopted.

"I decided to appeal to Rachael's intellect, which is a capable one. 'Rachael, let's think about that. Does that make any sense? How could the process of adoption make you not very bright? Adoption is simply being raised by parents who did not give birth to you. Tell me how that can make you smart or stupid?

"Could a child who was later adopted be born not-so-smart? Sure. But do you know any kids who were born into their families that are not-so-smart? Of course you do.

"What those girls said is just not true. Where they got such a strange idea I'm sure I don't know."

Rachael was thoughtful but didn't comment any further. Constance left it there, aching for her child upon whom such a ridiculous assumption had been heaped.

"It must have helped," Constance reported. "Rachael came home with a slightly triumphant air a few days later.

"They tried it again," she announced. "They said adopted kids are stupid. I told them that wasn't scientific. I told them adopted kids are just born like everyone else, sort of smart or sort of stupid, and it's how hard you work that makes you smarter or stupider from then on."

"Hooray!" Constance rejoined. "Rachael, it couldn't have been said better."

❖

Friends

Samantha: age twelve

Samantha was twelve, and so Helen held her breath but let her daughter handle the question when her friend said, "Was your real mother Jewish, too?"

"This *is* my real mother," Samantha replied with only a second's hesitation and without any embellishment.

She might have chosen a different response to that query, but on that particular day, this was her answer, and Helen felt no intervention was needed. Helen didn't know from her statement whether Samantha was establishing the fact that this was private information, that she didn't feel like having a discussion on the topic, or that she simply wanted to emphasize the bond between herself and her mom. Whatever her reasoning, Helen felt it was perfectly valid.

❖

Alex and Christy: ages eleven and twelve

The two families were quite good friends, and the adults had discussed adoption in different contexts a number of times during the two years since they had been acquainted as families. "It was probably this background and my assumptions that then left me surprised and speechless," Danielle said.

"Our family had been invited to have dinner with their family—something we had probably never done quite so formally with them before. Our two children were being uncharacteristically quiet at the table. Any

157

time we might have partied poolside or by a campfire in the past, all four children had been regular rowdy kids.

"This evening, however, the host children were chatting animatedly with the adults while our children looked on. Suddenly the older daughter of the house looked pointedly at our eleven-year-old son Alex and said, 'You don't talk as much as your mom and dad. Are you adopted or something?'

"The tone was not a negative one, just a teasing one. While the rest of us sat speechless, our son answered matter-of-factly, 'Yes, I am.'"

"Oh, really?"

A nodding of his head and a level gaze.

The girl's father saved the day with a quick observation. "But look, Christy, your mom's kind of quiet, and you're *certainly* not! There goes your theory."

It worked out fine. Danielle wished she'd been ready with a quick kid-level discussion of nature vs. nurture—a healthy subject for children to consider and a ploy which would have moved the subject away from the personal.

"I was pleased that my son was not thrown by the situation," Danielle concluded. "He had obviously not mentioned his adoption to these children, something he has a perfect right not to do. When it arose, however, he handled it without flinching. It seemed perfectly healthy and plucky to me."

❖

Chapter Eight

School

The most-often-asked question in any meeting of adoptive parents, especially parents whose children are young, is undoubtedly, "Do you tell your child's teacher that your child was adopted?" While there can be no absolute answer since, of course, personalities are involved, the following vignettes show how some parents have handled the issue.

The next-often-asked question concerning school and the adopted child is the one about The Family Tree. How do you help your child cope with it? How do you help the teachers handle it? A number of vignettes articulate the concerns of parents and include helpful suggestions.

These dialogues, arranged by the age of the child involved, come from interviews with parents of children in nursery school through middle school. Parents of children in upper school seemed to have more concerns about their children's peer interaction in school than about interaction with teachers regarding the subject of adoption.

❖

Marshall: age three

"Have you always told your children's teachers that your kids were adopted?" Mary asked.

"I do have some thoughts on that," Joyce answered. "My first experience wasn't such a good one. It's a long story, but just *don't* do what I did, whatever you do! When my son, Marshall, was three," she continued, " I found the perfect little easy-going nursery school for him, just three mornings a week. It was really the only one I liked for him, and so it wasn't as if I could just select another easily. Also, there seemed to be more children than spaces in nursery schools that year, and so I wanted to do this just right so that I was sure my son could attend that school.

"At any rate, the application for admission to the school arrived in the mail one day. I grabbed a pen and began filling in the blanks until I got halfway down the first sheet. There, front and center of page one was the question: 'Is your child adopted?' Followed by, 'Are any of his/her siblings adopted?'

"Now believe me, I'm so thrilled that we were able to adopt our son that I tell *everybody*. I probably talk about it too much. But suddenly I was faced with having the fact pulled out of me, and I didn't like the feeling.

"To my credit, I have since talked to the school about my feelings at that time, and they have incorporated into their admissions procedure the opportunity for parents to talk about adoption if they would like to. Now the question reads: 'Are there any circumstances of which you would like us to be aware regarding your child so that we can handle it well if the issue should arise? For example, are grandparents living with you? Is a new baby on the way? Was your child or sibling adopted? Has there been a recent divorce?'

"But back to my story. My husband was out of town and rather incommunicado at the time, and so I called a friend. She indignantly agreed that the question was out of line. Obviously we got a bit carried away, feeling I suppose that if the school could be inappropriate, so could I, and so when my friend said, 'Why don't you just lie?', I thought it was a great idea."

"Groan," Mary interjected.

"You're right. It was a lousy idea. But that's what I did. I found the same black pen and cheerfully wrote 'No' in the offensive blank.

"When school began, I realized, of course, that I couldn't talk about adoption to these moms or teachers. And remember, I was always one who talked too much! Pretty soon I found myself, even with friends outside of the school, trying to remember if any of them knew any of the moms in the school! It was a nightmare! I decided to play it out that year, and the next year we were changing schools anyway. Guess who was the first one to bring up adoption to the new teacher!

"But that's not necessarily what I advocate, either. Let's go back to the first nursery school. When I did talk to the director about my concern, she quickly understood and made appropriate changes. She said that they only ask because the children will often say they are adopted, and it seems to work more smoothly if the teacher knows if this is fact or fantasy. While it's usually older children who have adoption fantasies, the director said that a few children who had older adopted siblings would claim, even at three, that they were adopted too.

"And so I realized that this information would have been in good hands in this particular school. And that's what I learned to look for. My rule of thumb has become, especially while the child is in elementary school: Tell the teacher your child was adopted unless you have some gut reaction that tells you not to do so. And this can happen. Teachers like everyone in our society can have biases.

"When I talk to a teacher about adoption, I have learned to slip it in almost casually so as not to create the impression that this is some unpleasant piece of information about my child that automatically places him at risk or bears watching. It's not. It's simply a fact about my child that may come up in school and may affect some few assignments regarding family that may be asked of him. That's the reason for telling a teacher. There is no other reason.

"Now you want to know how to have an educated gut reaction, right? Probably the only tangible thing I can suggest is that you watch and listen to how the teacher reacts to and handles any child who is different in any way. A teacher who seems cold and uncaring to me doesn't get my vote.

"If that's your initial reaction but you later change your mind—you can bring up adoption later. 'Oh, yes, I keep meaning to tell you that we adopted Billy as an infant—in case he should bring it up in class' can be said at any time during the school year. Have some other comment about school ready to add, because people are sometimes at a loss as to how to respond to this bit of information. You are in effect educating them, implying that this is factual information and nothing more. It's not a red flag. It's not a concern. It's simply a fact."

❖

Paula: age six

"We adopted Paula from India when she was three," Lydia reminded her daughter's first-grade teacher. "We don't have any baby pictures for tomorrow's assignment, but I will send the flag of the country of Paula's birth, some pictures we took there, and the dress she wore to her new home in the United States."

The teacher was appropriately apologetic. She knew that Paula had come to the Nelson family only two years earlier. "It just didn't enter my mind," she said.

She more than made up for it a few weeks later. She called to say she had thought of having a weekly VIP day. Once a week, one of the children could, on Friday afternoon, bring whatever he thought he would like to share with classmates, anything he felt was special about himself. "Do you see any problems with the assignment?" she asked. "I don't want to goof again!"

Lydia suggested that there might be a problem with some children having parents available to come to share their special day and others not having that luxury. Perhaps no parents should come. "And," the teacher added, "I should probably call the child's home before his or her VIP day to be sure the parent understands and that no child feels left out."

Lydia thanked the teacher for the thoughtful assignment and thanked her for phoning. She assured the teacher that she was available at any time to discuss any assignment and to help brainstorm if alternative assignments were in order for any that might prove to be difficult for some children because of their backgrounds.

"I thought of another one I'd like to discuss with you sometime," the teacher continued. "I'd like to highlight the ethnic diversity in our classroom by having each child find out where his family or families originally came from. We could put little pins on a world map."

Lydia is a strong advocate of educating teachers about adoption instead of just being irritated if they make an insensitive assignment. "Why should we expect any more of teachers than we do of the general public when it comes to understanding adoption?" Lydia asks. "Unfortunately, this isn't something that's taught in teacher eduation classes. Teachers are a product of their society as is everyone else. Certainly you'll find a few whose insensitivity about adoption will never change, but for the most part, teacher's are willing and delighted to get input along these lines—when it's offered in a kind and helpful way. Make yourself available as a volunteer consultant. And don't worry about not knowing how! Brainstorming is just that, and who better than you can recognize an idea which will be considerate of your child's position. Jump in!"

❖

Jessie: age eight

The teacher had sounded slightly upset when she called that evening, and Ann soon learned why. Miss Dawson was a young teacher and was trying so hard to do everything right, but Ann reassured her this was not a question many teachers, no matter how experieced, would be asked to handle.

Jessie, now in third grade, had gone to her teacher and asked, "Miss Dawson, can you help me find my birthmother?"

Ann assured Miss Dawson she had done the right thing, recommending to Jessie that she talk to her parents about it. "I'm glad she talked to you, though, Miss Dawson. It shows how comfortable Jessie is with you. I really don't think she would have talked with many people about this subject."

❖

Renee: age eight

Bette had considered telling the teacher at Renee's new school that Renee was adopted, but the more she thought about it, the less need she could see for doing so.

The third grade teacher called that first afternoon. "You'll need to talk to your daughter," she began. "She's telling everyone at school that she was adopted."

"That's okay," Bette responded. "She was."

❖

Michael: age eleven

Ann tells of having told each of her son Michael's nursery school and primary school teachers that he was adopted—until her son reached fifth grade. That year there had been so much to talk about at the conference. The teacher had fascinating plans in store for the children, and Ann walked out the door at the end of the half hour and thought, "Good grief. I forgot to mention adoption!"

"I almost turned around and went back to the teacher," Ann says, "and then I realized I had probably forgotten about it because it had ceased to become so important for my son's teachers to know about it. He can handle things himself, now. The 'family tree assignment' is behind him. He's beyond the stage where his awareness of adoption caused him to talk about it to quite an extent. I'll just leave it alone," she decided.

"And it worked out fine. There was one composition, I happened to notice, in which Michael talked about his adoption and birthparents,"

Ann said. "But the teacher never called, and Michael never volunteered information about whether his teacher had mentioned it or not.

"When Michael entered sixth grade, I went to the parent conference planning to talk about adoption only if it seemed necessary or appropriate for some reason. Again it just never came up, and this year I left the classroom with no second thoughts.

"I learned from the mother of one of my son's classmates about the time it did come up during that sixth-grade year. It seems the teacher was encouraging the students to take a look at themselves, and the assignment involved answering dozens of personal questions ranging from the factual to the more abstract. One of the first questions was simply, 'Where were you born?'

"I think it threw him because that was one thing Michael had wanted to know, and though we have since found the answer for him, at that time he didn't know the place of his birth. The teacher happened to walk by Michael's desk, and realizing that Michael was stuck, looked down at his paper."

"Well, you know where you were born, don't you?" the teacher asked. Instead of giving an explanation, Michael just shook his head. "What?" the teacher continued. "You don't know where you were born?"

Michael's friend had jumped into the conversation. "No, he doesn't. He was adopted and that's why he doesn't know where he was born."

"Oh," the teacher had answered, not missing a beat. "Well, that's okay. Just leave it blank and go on."

Ann continued, "That's the chance you take if you don't tell the teacher about your child's adoption. On the other hand, probably most adopted kids know where they were born, and so the teacher's reaction may have been the same even if she had been told. And then, did this cause discomfort for Michael? If there was much discomfort, it was probably more related to the fact that he still didn't know where he was born than to the incident itself.

"It obviously caused some concern on the part of Michael's friend, who worried about it enough to relate it to his mother. She had called me, wondering if her son's action had been appropriate. I told her I thought it was wonderful that her son would help Michael out of what was probably an uncomfortable situation.

"Michael never brought the incident to my attention, and he usually would tell me what was on his mind. I used this bit of knowledge not to change my thoughts on whether it's important for teachers to know of a child's adoption—especially when the child is in the upper grades. I used it instead to remind myself that I had some calls to make, calls to find out where in fact Michael was born."

❖

Terin: age eleven

"Terin doesn't know anything about her biological family tree," Shelly said. "But even if she did, I'm not sure it's her school's perogative to suggest she include her biological background in that assignment. Have you ever heard of this being suggested to a sixth grader?" Shelly asked the consultant at her family's adoption agency.

"No, I've never heard of that happening before," Kaye replied. "Actually, this sounds like a pendulum swing to me. For so long, absolutely

no thought was given to adopted children when the family tree assignment was passed out. Now it may be that awareness has generated
hypersensitivity in the other direction."

"Shouldn't this decision ideally be left up to the child and her family?"
Shelly continued. "How can a teacher know if the timing is good for
this kind of inquiry and research."

"Most often, if properly handled, the assignment is left open for the
child who was adopted," Kaye replied. "If she brings up her adoption,
she is told she can talk it over with her family and decide if she'd like to
include family backgrounds of her adoptive family, her biological family, or both. Most assignments include a second tree connected by a
dotted line in case the child chooses to use it, but it is optional. Perhaps
you could suggest this when you talk to Terin's teachers.

"Some children, by the way, simply include their adoptive family without comment, one mother I know learned after the fact. Her child's
teacher wasn't aware that Casey had been adopted, and Casey chose
that year to leave it that way. Another year she may have wanted to turn
over heaven and earth to find answers. But it really is important that it
be the child's choice, that she be allowed to conduct her life in her own
way regarding exploration of her origins."

❖

Anya: age twelve

Marion wonders if teachers are aware of how many strong emotions
they may be tapping into when they discuss family trees with children
in divorced families or children who were adopted.

"Teachers may not realize that some parents will have very strong feelings about how and with whom these issues are broached, mainly because they want to be sure they are dealt with in an appropriate way. One parent told me of a sex education teacher who was questioned by a sixth-grade student about what happens when a girl who is not married becomes pregnant. As the teacher explained the various choices the girl would have, she ended with, 'Or the young woman could choose to place the child for adoption so that the child would be raised by someone who was ready to parent.'"

"Another child in the class reacted. 'That's horrible! How could anyone give away her kid? That should never happen.'

"The teacher noted out of the corner of her eye the reaction of a girl in the class, Anya, whom she knew had been adopted. To her credit, the teacher called Anya's parents and explained what had happened. But, unfortunately, she didn't handle the incident at the time. She really wasn't equipped to deal with this issue, and how many classroom teachers are? That's not where their training lies, and so I'm not criticizing them. I'm simply saying they may not know what they're getting into when they delve into anyone's family tree in this day and age.

❖

Adult to adult

Sybil was telling her friend Debra about the elaborate family tree assignment her sixth-grade daughter had received. "This one was a joint project between my daughter's homeroom teacher and her science teacher, and so I'm sure they're stressing actual genetics. I think I'm going to suggest that they could use other ways to achieve their objectives, using plants or animals."

169

"I wonder," her friend Debra remarked, "if the teachers realize how difficult or nearly impossible it is for many of our adopted children to produce a geneology of their birthparents. Often families are lucky even to know ethnic origins. Teachers may not be aware of this.

"You bring up an interesting point in assuming the objective of the assignment is the teaching of genetics. It makes me curious about where this particular assignment had it's origins," Debra continued. "I can imagine that illustrating genetics with the nuclear family might have been simple in the fifties. Today, I would venture to say family structure is just too complicated to be a very effective medium to use in achieving this goal."

"And at times, teaching genetics may not be the goal at all," Sybil said. "Perhaps the goal is to prove some point about ethnicity—a first-hand look at the United States as a melting pot, for instance. In that case there could be gentle ways to proceed that would allow every child to participate and yet not face any unnecessary pressures. Each child, for example, could be given the assignment of bringing to class the name of one country in which any member of his family has his roots. Everyone could contribute, and the array of pins on the world map would indeed make a statement."

❖

Adult to adult

"I've heard of children reacting in so many different ways to the family tree assignment," Shirl began. "One child I heard about actually fabricated a family tree, evidently thinking, correctly or not, that she had to produce her biological tree in order to get a grade. We don't want children put into this situation. Undoubtedly the teacher would have been horrified to realize that the student felt she was being forced into this position—but that's what can happen when teachers innocently delve into this subject. They can't know which child is too sensitive even to approach the teacher and explain the difficulty.

"A friend of mine, a woman whose children are now in high school, told me once of some fabricating she herself had done as a student in order to save face. The assignment was a seemingly non-threatening one. The students were simply to list the foods that they ate during one week—breakfasts, lunches, dinners, and snacks—so that the class could discuss healthy diets. My friend says she'll never forget being embarrassed to write what she actually ate for those seven dinners—because her family was so poor that the fare was a humiliating one to parade before the class. And so she looked at a classmate's paper and copied 'steak, leg of lamb, and shrimp,' some of which she'd never seen in her life! The incident has stayed with her all these years, and that was only *food*, for goodness sake."

Shirl's friend Mary Ann added, "Think of the child who is asked to list his family status ... if a divorce is imminent or recent, if the child lives with a single parent and has never met the missing parent, if he was adopted and has concerns about this very issue. Think of how confusing it might be for the child who is wondering if his father is still his father since he doesn't live at home anymore. And to whom will that child go for comfort and answers? His mother may be in turmoil herself and seem unapproachable to the child.

"Issues of loss, of sadness, of confusion can so easily lurk just beneath the surface for so many children today. The person who opens those issues has a responsibility, it seems to me, to be able to handle them."

"I agree," Shirl added. "And so while this assignment might be nearly impossible for the child who was adopted, it's quite likely that it might

171

be painful for a large number of the children in any given class. Many children might have a very difficult time, emotionally, drawing the various families and stepfamilies on a chart. I wonder if we wouldn't be doing half the children in the class a favor by reminding the teachers of today's variety of family situations and of how the children might be less than comfortable displaying them before the class. Certainly the assignment could be offered, but possibly to be done optionally at home with parents."

❖

Chapter Nine
Dealing With The World

Most parents and children, thankfully, will live their entire lives without having words said to them that are as hurtful as those contained in some of the following anecdotes. The stories are shared simply so that adoptive parents can be aware that there are a few cruel and thoughtless people in the world, and so that parents can give some thought to how they would react if the truly horrendous were to be said and was heard by their children.

The dialogues in this section, then, have been included with a degree of hesitancy. First, if children can be spared these hurtful words, they should be, and putting them into a book makes them more accessible to children, even if the book is not intended for them. In addition, will inclusion of these stories over-emphasize a negative attitude toward adoption? Most negative comments are inadvertent and probably reflect a societal bias of which the offending individual is largely unaware. These particular anecdotes, however, for the most part reflect overt bias—but a bias that is relatively rare.

On the other hand, a bit of preparation can help a person who has the misfortune of being confronted with a negative comment to be, if not prepared for it, at least not devastated by it. Knowing that bias exists but is quite rare can put it into perspective. The person can know that he has faced an unfortunate but unusual incident. He can know that some such incidents can be handled, and that there is nothing to do but walk away from others.

Perhaps more importantly, awareness of the fact that overt and unconscious biases still do exist in this country may prepare adoptive parents to deal effectively with biases, large or small, whenever they are encountered. Awareness is the first step toward countering bias and makes inclusion of the unpleasant necessary. Those parents who dislike confrontation may gain needed courage through these vignettes. Those ready for battle may find effective words to use.

Just as the age and stage of the child involved have been important in every aspect dealt with in earlier chapters of this book, they are crucial here, as is suggested by the words of a speaker at a recent conference on adoption held in Washington, DC.

"What should we do with intrusive questions or unkind comments?" the speaker was asked.

"It depends so much on the circumstance," she replied. "Parents work out for themselves what is best for their family.

"But there is one rule-of-thumb: If your child is with you when the question or comment is made, your answer must be made with your child in mind and not at all for the satisfaction of the stranger."

And so what do parents do? They do what they think is best for their child at the moment, and, if possible, try to educate later. The following dialogues are examples of the painful incidents that occasionally occur and illustrate the various ways that parents handled the situations.

❖

Timmy: age two

"This is our son Timmy, who just came to live with us," Jane said as she greeted her friend Kim at the door. "Timmy has a new truck to show you."

"Wow, what a great truck!" Jane exclaimed as she examined Timmy's offering. "Do you have any other toys?"

Kim followed two-year-old Timmy, who ran ahead to the playroom, pointing the way. She knelt by Timmy and received each car and truck he gave her. And then he was off to the swing set with his big brother and a friend from across the street.

"Thank you," Jane said when she and Kim were alone.

"You're welcome. But what am I being thanked for?" Kim asked.

"For not asking about Timmy's background—especially not in front of him. You won't believe how many people ask what happened, why we got him now, while Timmy is standing right there. It's as if they think he can't understand what they're saying. Granted, he may not be talking much yet, but he *certainly* understands."

"Not to mention it's nobody's business—whether Timmy is present or not—unless you feel like explaining," Kim added. "I'd be furious. What on earth do you say?"

"The best we've been able to come up with is 'Oh, Timmy needed us now.' That's true, and it's okay for Timmy to hear. People so far have taken the hint and haven't asked more."

Samantha: age four

"I'm sure it's the impact of our location," Molly explained. "We live in a small, rather isolated town in New England. While Dan, who is Caucasian, too, and I would certainly choose to live in an integrated community, there just isn't one. And so our daughter Samantha, who was born in Cambodia, is not only the minority here. She is in fact the only person of color in the whole town."

Molly had just had a second horrible experience, and that was enough. She simply had to find another school for Samantha, who had just turned four.

The first incident had occurred when Molly was picking Sammie up from nursery school at noon and was chatting with the teacher's aide while Sammie and the other children continued to play for a few more minutes on the playground equipment. Suddenly Sammie ran full speed up to Molly and said, all out of breath, "Mommy, can you make my braids tighter, quick, so I can play some more." Molly laughed as she tightened the braids but quit laughing abruptly as the aide said, in an evident attempt at humor, "Sammie, maybe that's why your eyes are so squinty. You have your braids too tight."

"This probably doesn't have anything to do with adoption. I know it's pure and simple racial insensitivity," Molly said. "And yet I have this sense that the aide would not have said such a thing if I had been Asian like my daughter."

Molly went home and called the lead teacher, who said certainly her aide meant no harm, but that she would talk to her about it. "People can learn and grow," Molly reasoned.

It came as a shock to Molly, then, when a few weeks later she was again waiting for Sammie on the playground and again chatting with the same aide. Once again, Sammie appeared, out of breath, but this time wanting to go home quickly. Once again, Molly laughed. "Sammie's in the I-only-want-to-use-my-own-bathroom stage," she said as the two of them started for the car.

"Sammie," the aide called after them. "Maybe that's why your skin is so yellow. You need to go to the bathroom more often."

Molly felt the only thing she could do in response to the situation was turn and slowly walk away. A high-valence reaction on her part might, she thought, have made the incident more damaging for Samantha.

Was she right? Should she have spoken out, in front of her daughter? Molly keeps mulling the incident over in her mind, still not sure.

Shaking with rage all the way home, Molly did the things she knew to do. After phoning the lead teacher, she found a new school for her daughter. She is beginning the arduous task of educating teachers about adoption, especially interracial adoption. She's bringing appropriate books to the schools, all the schools, and to teachers' lounges. She's trying to find speakers for in-service training since she's found one sympathetic principal. She's doing what she can "behind the scenes," attempting to keep herself and Samantha from being the focus. She's also telling Samantha that people in this town just don't know much about adoption and people from other countries, and that it would be nice to help them learn.

❖

Analise: age twelve

Jane had explained to the pediatrician that since she and her husband
had adopted Analise, she didn't know if her slight curvature of the spine
was hereditary. She explained to the allergist that since Analise was
adopted, allergies that might have been inherited were not known. And
she had explained to the ophthalmologist that, since she had adopted
Analise, her own near-sightedness was irrelevant.

And then the time came to see the orthodontist. Analise had a slight
space between her front teeth. Should it be corrected, or would subsequent molars make the gap disappear?

The orthodontist's question irritated Jane. "Did you or your husband
have braces?"

Why should that matter? Some children have perfectly straight teeth
while their biological siblings do not. And so Jane replied, "That's not
relevant."

"Of course it is," the orthodontist said, surprised.

"Well," Jane continued, "I'm going to ask you to make a decision about
my daughter's teeth, to decide whether Analise needs braces or not,
without that piece of information."

❖

Rebecca: age fourteen

The discussion had centered on whether the adopted status of a person
was an appropriate detail to be mentioned in news articles. "Unless it's

actually germane to the issue, and it seldom is, I think it's ridiculous to include," Nora, an adoptive parent, insisted.

"But what if it's positive information that's being reported, maybe about a famous person who was adopted. Doesn't that promote positive feelings about adoption?" Nora's friend Rita asked.

"Probably," Nora agreed, "but I don't think we can have it both ways. In fact, it makes me think of the Olympics several years ago. The commentator, with the best of intentions, decided to highlight the fact that a large number of the contestants were persons who had been adopted. At first, it seemed nice, and then it got to be tedious and slightly embarrassing. Reporters relentlessly asked mothers to confirm the adopted status of their children, and what really was there for them to say but 'Yes.' Perhaps I was projecting my own feelings, but I kept sensing that they wanted to add 'So?' but were too polite to do that."

Nora's daughter Rebecca, who had just turned fourteen and who had been adopted as an infant, interrupted at that point. "I remember that, too. I kept waiting for them to ... to make a point. Of course, I was just a little kid then."

"Little kid or not, you got it right!" Nora exclaimed. "I know the intentions were good, but what message was actually coming across? That adopted kids, even a preponderance of them, might grow up to be stars? Well, of course they might. It's almost demeaning to have made an issue of it. That particular year many Olympians happened to have been adopted as children. Four years later, that wasn't the case. So?

"Of course," Nora continued, "this example is pretty benign. But the problem is—if we encourage or allow non-germane mention of adoption in a case like this, then we become accustomed to having it highlighted. And so then when the occasional person who was adopted becomes a criminal, as will certainly happen since there are 5 million adopted persons in this country, we allow his adopted status to be pointed out. Most people don't even notice the inequity since they've become accustomed to the phrase 'adopted son of Mr. and Mrs. Jones.'

"Equality would demand that a similar phrase be included with the name of every other criminal in every other news article: 'biological son of Mr. and Mrs. Jones.' If a criminal's method of entering his family were noted in *every* case, then adoption would be put into perspective. As it stands now, serial killer Son of Sam is always the adopted son of his parents, but Jeffrey Dahmer and Ted Bundy, it is never stated, were born into their families."

"It should be like the race of a person," Rebecca interrupted again. "We talk about this in school all the time. It's not right to point out the race of a minority person who was arrested. It gives people the wrong idea— as if that whole race is a bunch of criminals."

"Exactly," Nora agreed. "That's a perfect analogy. And you're right about how powerful that subtle linkage can be. It doesn't take too many of those stories until 'adopted equals criminal' in the minds of readers.

"What can we do? Write to reporters and to editors and to movie producers, educating them about the need for germaneness. Most have never thought about it in connection with adoption. And, yes, Rebecca, 14-year-olds *can* write letters to the editor!"

❖

Ian and Kassandra: teens

George's family had been invited to the home of friends for dinner. The grandmother, a woman who voiced her opinion on every subject, was visiting from out of town. She joined the group in the living room before dinner, and when the subject of adoption arose in connection with George's teenage son and daughter, Ian and Kassandra, who were present, Grandma proceeded to insult them and all adopted persons, belittling their parentage, their personhood, and their prospects, all very tersely and articulately.

George could hardly believe his ears, and so it took him a few minutes to react. When he did react, what popped out was, "You're talking pure rubbish, lady, and you'd better shut your mouth before I put my foot in it." At which point the hostess escorted the family to the door, herself appropriately apologetic.

George's angry reaction told his children that he would always be there for them and assured them that the words being uttered were in fact utter nonsense.

❖

Adult to adult

Connie had clipped the syndicated column out of the newspaper and taped it to her mirror. "It's the perfect rejoinder to the intrusive question," she explained. "Turn the tables with the query, 'Why do you ask?'

"Sometimes, in fact," Connie continued, "the question is based on more than mere curiosity. One woman in a grocery store became teary as she answered, 'Oh, my husband and I would like to adopt, and we just can't seem to get anywhere.'

"More often, in my experience, the question 'Where did your child come from?' is asked out of idle curiosity. This question I answer matter-of-factly, but there I usually draw the line. I view any other question about my child's background as inappropriate.

"This questioning happened frequently when my daughter was quite young. I always did a gracious side step and hoped the person would catch on. 'Oh, we were lucky. Our agency had a lot of data to pass on to us,' I would answer to the query of 'What do you know about her background?'

"Usually the person did catch on. An abrupt change of the subject was next on my list. But always there and available was the question I was grateful to have at my disposal: 'Why do you ask?' Somehow it gave me a mind-set, a realization that some things are private, and I need feel no obligation to answer."

❖

Adult to adult

"We've not seen him for seven years," Jack said, "and it looks like that's the way it will stay."

Fortunately the children were already in bed when the incident occurred. Jack's brother had been in town on business, just overnight, and was not spending the night, only having dinner with them. He'd evidently had too much to drink, but his words still must have expressed feelings he was harboring.

"I don't know how you do it," he began as Sherri returned to the dining room table after putting the children to bed. "Amazing. You take two kids from heaven-only-knows what background into your home. How can you possibly love someone who's not your own flesh and blood?"

Jack ushered his brother unceremoniously to the door and said he'd be welcome in their house again only when those feelings changed.

❖

Adult to adult

It was a small dinner party of good friends. Dotty and Ed were announcing that their baby would soon arrive. Champagne flowed and appropriate parent jokes were exchanged.

But then Trent became serious. He was choosing his words carefully in an effort to avoid being rude. "In fact, I admire you. I'm not being critical. But I really don't think I could do it. How can you adopt a kid? How can you love a kid who's not your own blood?"

"Excuse me," Ed answered, choosing a bit of humor on this occasion. "You're not thinking clearly about families, Trent. You do love your wife, correct? Maybe I'm missing something, but I don't think you're related by blood to her, are you?"

❖

Adult to adult

"I guess you'd have to call me an activist where adoption is concerned," began Tracy. "I'd never written a letter to the editor in my life until we adopted our son. But now, every time I see an article which refers to someone's 'adopted son' who was in an accident, for example, and in the next paragraph, a child who was born into a family is not referred to as such, I dust off my Smith Corona and ask the newspaper or magazine for equal treatment. Whenever a children's Saturday-morning cartoon contains a disparaging remark about adoption, which is quite often, out comes the typewriter again.

"What concerns me is that the typewriter seems to be in constant use these days. Maybe I'm just attuned to them now and that's why they seem so numerous, but the inaccurate and negative comments about adoption seem to be everywhere. I started wondering why. I had heard a speaker suggest that our attitudes about adoption as a nation probably grew out of the British common law, upon which our laws are based, and England did not recognize adoption until 1926. So a child adopted in the United States faces that legacy, the historical feelings on the part of society that adoption is somehow second-class.

"Even with that knowledge, I worried that there might be something more. I searched my soul to see if within me there was any reservation about adoption, reservations which might apply to other people as well.

"What I finally found was a vague guilt about my initial reaction to adoption, to the fact that I cried, both of us cried, when we learned that we probably would never bear a child, and when we talked about adoption as a possibility. And that's probably true of every couple who has chosen adoption for this reason—realizing there are other reasons for choosing adoption, too.

"Does that mean we now think of adoption as second best? Absolutely not. What we experienced for those unspeakably difficult weeks or months was a mourning. We had experienced, in effect, a death of a child we had so wanted. But we made it through that period. And then any adoptive parent can speak of the incredible excitement of looking forward to the adoption.

"At this point, to get back to the original concern, we must ask two questions. The first is this. Would we have looked forward with more positive anticipation to that first child had we been birthing a child? Some adoptive parents have experienced both the birth of a child and the adoption of a child and can answer that question easily. Most adoptive parents have to take our word for it. The answer is: absolutely not. They are different experiences. Of course they're different. But is one filled with more positive anticipation than the other? No.

"And then there's the second crucial question. Could we possibly love our child more if he had been born into our family rather than enter our lives through adoption? That question can be answered best with another question. 'Are you kidding?' In fact, it sounds positively silly now that it's said.

"There's a tangential question that needs to be asked. Is there any adoptive parent who was unable to conceive that doesn't wish to have experienced pregnancy? I would guess that most do. And would it have been nice if our child that we adopted had been born to us? Probably so. It would have made many things easier as we look back over our lives.

"But look carefully at the question. The question was—would it have been nice if *our child* had been born to us. *Our child.* This child. Probably most people who have not given birth would prefer to do so. But there is no wish to substitute any experience of birth for *our child,*

185

and the desire is not accompanied by that desperation we felt about the possibility of never having a family, the desperation that disappeared when our child was placed in our arms.

"And so we all know that adoption is not second best. Adoption is simply one of the ways of building a family."

❖

Adult to adult

"I know people mean well. I know they're trying to show us we have something in common. But I wish they'd quit. I get tired of being introduced as an adoptive mother at every luncheon where there's even one other adoptive mother," Saundra said.

"A new acquaintance and I will discover that about each other soon enough if it's relevant to anything," she continued. "Otherwise, there's really no harm in letting it lie."

"It's like the newspaper always mentioning if a person is adopted," Eleanora agreed.

"Speaking of newspapers," Saundra added, "when I die, if anyone writes in my obituary 'survived by her husband and her adopted daughter,' I promise you I will come back to haunt them!"

❖

Dealing With The World

Adult to adult

Dianne hadn't talked to anyone other than her mother and her best friend about the fact that she and her husband had decided on adoption. It was easier that way. She was afraid people would keep asking about their progress with the agency, and Dianne knew herself well enough to know she could easily get teary. Why not just wait until it happened and then shout "Surprise!" from the rooftops.

But then one day she told another friend and evidently that friend had not sensed the private nature of Dianne's confidence. And so it happened that, shortly thereafter, at a luncheon, a not-so-subtle acquaintance with a not-so-subtle voice approached Dianne. "Well, did you get the call yet?" she fairly shouted.

"Pardon me?" Dianne queried, not because she hadn't heard but because she hadn't understood.

"Sara says you're adopting a baby. Did you get the call yet?" the woman repeated in her 'I'm going to get credit for being the first to know' voice.

Dianne, taken aback that something so insensitive could happen, simply mumbled, "No, not yet," and quickly excused herself and headed for the iced tea table.

"How could this have happened?" she pondered. "Do people perhaps not realize the emotion involved, the hurts, the heartbreaks, the fears, the difficult waiting? It's just not quite like saying 'When is the baby due?' It's so much more complicated. Certainly some people, and I envy them, are strong enough to announce their intentions to the world

187

ahead of time. But those of us who aren't should be able to expect a bit of understanding. I don't think I'm being overly sensitive. I think people simply need to be educated."

It was too late for that particular exchange, but Dianne would be ready for subsequent comments. "Oh, I guess we just aren't talking much about it yet" would be a polite way of saying, "This in not something I care to discuss with you at this point." Were the woman to pursue the subject, which probably would not happen, the iced tea excuse would always be appropriate.

Unfortunately, this was not the end of Dianne's discomfort that day. Word had spread quickly, of course, and suddenly another woman appeared at Dianne's side, a stranger to her. Certainly with the best of intentions the woman explained that she was herself both an adoptive and biological mother, and all was well, and congratulations to Dianne, and so forth. But then she added ominously, "I feel I have to warn you. My friends adopted through Agency X, too, and they waited over two years for their child."

The tears came, all right, and so needlessly. Do we rush in to tell our friend who is soon to undergo delicate back surgery about other back-surgery failures we know about, or do we concentrate on the successful ones? Unless we're our friend's primary confidant, do we pry into marital situations or other personal matters?

If the woman needed to pass on the unpleasant fact that this particular agency were a disreputable one, then the information would be appropriate even though unpleasant. But Dianne was only too aware of the waiting period. Short of privacy, encouragement was in order.

❖

Adult to adult

"I haven't been very open in telling people that we adopted our children," Sue said. "I had a bad experience with a neighbor the second week after Matthew joined our family, and I guess it made me cautious.

"I didn't know many people in the neighborhood at the time. We hadn't lived there long, and I'd been working full-time downtown, not to mention doing paperwork for the adoption!

"I had decided to quit my job and be home with Matthew, and I was outside with him on a sunny spring day. An older woman two doors down was gardening that morning, and so I stopped to chat.

"Since I had not been seen pregnant in the neighborhood, I thought it was logical that I explain the fact that we had adopted Matthew."

"Adopted?" the woman repeated. "Oh, oh. You might have real trouble. You don't know what's gotten passed on to him. You might have a criminal on your hands."

"Needless to say, I decided announcing Matthew's adoption to the rest of the community was unnecessary. Shortly thereafter, we found a house in a neighborhood that we loved, and so we moved and I have never again seen the woman.

"In the new neighborhood, I made a conscious decision to avoid paranoia but still be relatively cautious about discussing adoption. Actually it's worked out pretty well for us. We talk about it with people who become friends, of course, and I usually tell this story so that they will understand why I didn't bring it up earlier. We're open about it with our

children—Matthew's sister arrived two years later—and they have always felt free to discuss it with whom they choose.

"As I said, it's worked for our family. I will never forget, though, the
absolute horror I felt when I realized that stereotyping of this magnitude
still existed in the minds of some people toward adopted persons."

❖

Adult to adult

Sally was furious.

It had been one of those difficult days. Jon had been out of town on
business for the better part of the week. The mom who was scheduled
to drive the car pool had a sick child, and Sally couldn't leave the house
to take Jackie to preschool because the furnace repairman was going to
show up supposedly sometime between 9 a.m. and noon.

Jackie, though three, was still able to display a two-year-old tantrum
and had chosen to do so when he learned he couldn't attend nursery
school that morning. And Erin's ear was still bothering her, even though
she was on an antibiotic. She kept pulling at her ear, her only method of
conveying discomfort at age one, in addition to the crying.

Sally was coping. She would have made it. It was hard, of course, but
the anger didn't hit until the phone call.

Grandma called from Palm Springs. Just a chatty little call. Sally took
the occasion to unload a bit. Not to complain, exactly, but just to share
and receive the expected supportive pat on the back through the telephone line.

But that wasn't quite what she got.

"My own mother," Sally fairly screamed into the phone an hour later to her friend Susan, "my own mother said, 'Well, Sally, you asked for it.'

"Can you believe it? I guess an adoptive mother just doesn't have the right to have a bad day."

❖

Adult to adult

They were all adult women, and all had been adopted as infants or small children. They were concerned about media portrayal of adoption, and they had decided to meet a few times each year to decide what they could do about the negative stereotyping of adopted persons.

They were recounting with laughter some of the experiences they had personally encountered when Dana said, "You know, we're so concerned about biases in the media, but let me tell you what my own mother said to me once.

"Now understand, we love each other dearly, but she'd evidently heard some negative stereotyping from some ill-informed speaker. My mother always attended meetings, bless her heart, with speakers who claimed to be authorities on adoption. We talked about her faux pas a few years ago, and she said she'd heard it referred to enough times that she assumed it was correct.

"I was a freshman in college, my first time away from home for any extended period, and I guess I was a bit thrown by the newness of it all. I realized near the end of the first quarter that, although my other grades were fine, I was going to receive a D in physics, and in high school I'd never gotten a grade lower than a B.

"I thought I'd call my mom and cushion the blow before the grades came in the mail. She wouldn't be upset, but she'd probably worry about me since a poor grade was so uncharacteristic.

"Mom," I began the phone conversation, "I've got really bad news."

"Oh, no! You're pregnant!"

"My mother told me later that the words had just slipped out, so fearful had she been of early pregnancy for me all those years."

Sadly, Dana wasn't the only one of the women to whom something similar had happened. They could laugh about it now, but it hadn't felt so good then.

❖

Adult to adult

"I hear you have a new baby! Congratulations!" Elise's friend called over the heads of several people at the children's soccer game.

"Yes!" Elise called back. "She's a honey."

"How old is she now?" her friend continued the conversation amidst the cheering.

"Six weeks. She's sleeping through the night!"

Elise could sense a woman behind her, a total stranger, scrutinizing her from head to toe. "You did *not* have a baby," the woman interrupted in an oddly angry voice. "You adopted one."

Elise simply turned away. "What on earth?" she thought, one-liner retorts flying through her head. "What's with this woman? What does our method of building a family have to do with anything? Why her anger? Is she a disgruntled adopted person? Had she tried to adopt and been unsuccessful?" Elise avoided the woman and hurriedly left when the game was over.

She phoned her friend Robin after she got home. "You'll never guess the weird thing that just happened to me," she said, recounting the incident.

Robin thought for a moment, pictured Elise's very slim figure, and asked, "Elise, was the woman heavyset herself?"

Elise laughed. "That did occur to me. Yes, she was." Elise and Robin, both very slim, had discussed once before how both had been the recipients of confusing, angry comments from women who evidently envied their figures. Hard as it was to believe, each had been told of the resentment harbored by some women who have a difficult time maintaining the weight they'd prefer.

"The subject wasn't even adoption, I'll bet," Elise concluded. "That's probably all it was. She just didn't think it was fair that I had a baby and a figure. And who am I to talk. I remember feeling sad, and maybe even angry, now that I think about it, when I'd see a pregnant woman— and I couldn't conceive. It's still a strange way for this woman to express it, but at least I didn't react defensively about adoption."

❖

Adult to adult

Rose looked up from the newsletter for adoptive parents that had just arrived in the mail. "I'm really not comfortable with some of the articles about adopted kids," she commented to her husband. "The statistics they rely on seem irrefutable, but something doesn't feel right. They usually come from therapists who are helping patients who were adopted find answers to some of the puzzling aspects of their lives. The problem seems to be that it's assumed that this pattern can be applied to every person who was adopted. It bothers me. How can an extrapolation be made from a clinical situation to the general population—in this case the general population of adopted kids?"

"In a valid study," Paul, a mathematician, said, "children who are adopted need to be matched socio-economically and educationally, for example, with children born to their families. It would be very interesting to see, in such a study, how the children compare in terms of the numbers that have learning disabilities, the numbers that need the help of a therapist, and the numbers that really need to be in mental health institutions.

"By the way, those are the numbers that have always bothered me. There *are* proportionally more adopted persons in mental health institutions and more receiving outpatient help from therapists than the population warrants."

"Don't forget that we added to those statistics, Paul," Rose said.

Their daughter Lise had been badly traumatized at just under one year of age. The effects had not been too noticeable until nursery school time. Lise, always the out-going and gregarious baby, slowly had become a clinger. When left at the three-morning-a-week nursery school, Lise had to literally be peeled off Rose's legs. She didn't cry, but it was rare that she would engage in the happenings of the low-keyed, gentle nursery school.

Rose and Paul had talked with a psychologist about Lise's behavior, and together with the teachers, they tried a few bribes and behavior modification, and with some success. This gave them hope that Lise could learn to cope without direct intervention. They all decided on a more directed nursery school for the next year, wanting to see if that approach would help.

It didn't. Lise, in fact, dug in her heels and refused any interaction with the teacher. While she made some friends with whom she played during free times, it was evident rather quickly that she was not going to cooperate with the teacher. Interestingly, she was learning, since at home in the afternoon she would show her mother much of what the class had been doing in the morning. Rose and Paul felt some help was needed. They didn't waste any time interviewing the therapists who were recommended to them and starting therapy for Lise.

"But remember, Lise wasn't the only child of concern in that classroom of 16 children. There were two others that needed help probably more than Lise did. Remember one little boy who never came out from under the table?" Rose reminisced. "I know what you're saying. Those two little boys were born into their families. They didn't get professional help, and so they aren't statistics. We got help for Lise, whom we adopted, and now Lise is a statistic. One more adopted child who needed therapy.

"I don't mean to comment here on whether or not those little boys should have had any help. I'm just looking at the statistics that resulted. I've always dismissed the rather condescending suggestions that adoptive parents are exceptionally conscientious. But when you look at the combination of descriptors about adoptive parents—generally higher income levels and higher education levels, not to mention being hooked into the 'system' already after having gone through adoption—you may well have people who would be more inclined to seek help, and perhaps more quickly than most."

Paul added, "You realize the other statistic we've added to here. Lise's need for therapy had nothing to do with her adoption. In this case it was obvious, but how often is an assumption made that an adopted child's difficulty is adoption-related when in fact it may be related to something else: to physical deprivation as an infant, to the child's brilliance, to genetic factors that would become evident no matter who raised him, to the fact that the family moved many times during the child's younger years, to parenting mistakes. We must distinguish what is an adoption-related issue and what is not, or we will be vulnerable to every suggestion that comes along."

❖

Adult to adult

"Does adoption cause attention deficits? Does adoption cause emotional impairment? Does adoption cause separation anxieties? Does adoption cause learning disabilities?" Marjorie asked her friend Jane, a psychiatric social worker.

"I think the questions need to be restated before we tackle this subject," Jane responded. "'Does adoption cause...' is an easy, catch-all phrase, and the exact question really needs to be defined. It's very easy, if a preponderance of adopted children display certain tendencies, to jump to the conclusion that *adoption* caused them.

"The truth is, the concerns you listed could easily have been with that child, whether he had been raised by birthparents or adoptive parents. What have to be looked at are other mitigating circumstances, low birth weight, for example, possible genetic causes, neglect or abuse of the child after birth, poor parenting either on the part of birthparents or adoptive parents. What is the result of preexisting factors and what is the result of the actual act of adoption. In other words, might the child have had these same difficulties no matter who raised him?

"Valid research," Jane continued, "which would give conclusive answers to these and many more questions is extremely difficult to conduct because of the number of variables involved. No one, at this point in time, can say with absolute surety that adoption does or does not contribute to these and other problems. Some research that does exist seems flawed in that it does not distinguish between children adopted as infants and older-child placements. Even the seemingly conclusive data regarding the numbers of adopted children who receive professional counseling may be misleading. Adoptive parents may simply seek help more readily than do their counterparts.

"The pendulum keeps swinging between nature and nurture, as it has for decades. Most professionals currently seem to feel that certain tendencies may indeed be inherited and that environment may tip the balance in some situations.

"For our purposes," noted Jane, "it doesn't really matter. What any parent needs to do with any child, adopted or born into the family, who is in difficulty is help the child.

"Getting started seems to be the hard part. When is intervention needed? And by whom? Is this really a difficulty that needs addressing, or just a phase? These are some of the questions parents ask.

"There are many ways to begin," the social worker continued. "First, take stock of whom you know that might be helpful. A friend who is a counselor, a parent whose child has had similar difficulties, a parent support group. Adoption agencies often have a list of good resource persons.

"And then go ahead and talk to someone. That can never be a mistake, although it's probably wise to speak with a therapist who has dealt with a number of adopted children over the years. The reason is that it's easy to happen upon a therapist who is totally untrained in this area and who may find pathology where there is none. And then it's a good idea to use your own common sense when you interview possible therapists. If the therapist, even though experienced with adopted children, tends to blame *everything* on adoption, you may want to look further.

"If you talk to an understanding therapist and find, in fact, that your child's difficulty is part of a developmental stage, no harm has been done. If, on the other hand, you find that intervention is needed, you are lucky to have caught it early. Individual testing can help illuminate the situation, and generally the earlier the intervention, the better.

"A helpful and often comforting channel is a parent support group. There seem to be support groups now for virtually every condition imaginable. People in a group can be very helpful. Often a suggestion of a perfect specialist can come from a member. There are the obvious benefits of meeting other people who are dealing with a similar situation, although over-involvement can gobble up your time!

"Genes versus environment. It's the oldest argument where parenting is concerned. But does it matter in the long run? Let's assume that your parenting skills are adequate. Still, if there are things you can do to help your child with his difficulty, certainly you will want to know. Your child was assuredly born with certain tendencies. Still, if he can be assisted in overcoming a difficulty, surely you will want to avail him of the aid.

"And so, is adoption 'to blame' for any of the difficulties? Some problems seem to follow. The child with separation problems may have fear that was deepened by that initial separation from his birthmother. But how many children who are born into their families also have separation anxieties? How many children who were adopted don't? Once again, the argument seems pointless for our purposes here, because the real question is, will you treat the child differently if the fear is caused by adoption than you would if it had another cause? The child still needs to learn that mother will return. If the fear is severe, therapy may be needed. This is true whatever the origin of the cause and whatever the origin of the child.

"General advice can be given, advice which is invaluable when your child, adopted or born into your family, is in difficulty, and whether or not you decide seeing a specialist is in order:

1. Affirm your child whenever you can. He needs to know he is valued and must see that he is capable in some areas.

2. Don't engage in casual discussion of the problem in the presence of your child or his siblings or friends.

3. Understand child development. Some of the behavior about which you are worrying may be normal development.

4. Spend one-on-one time together daily. And have fun!

5. Allow your child to assume as much responsibility as possible. Trust his ability.

6. Listen to your child. Drop what you are doing and give full attention, particularly to the adolescent, who may not give you these opportunities often, and even if the topic is not your favorite.

7. Set reasonable limits.

8. Allow your child the freedom to make his own decisions whenever possible.

9. Correct misbehavior gently.

10. And most of all, accept your child for who he is. No child, however he enters the family, deserves to have a disappointed parent."

❖

Chapter Ten

A Call to Action

Biases toward adoption, large or small, overt or unintentional, need to be dealt with by adoptive parents whenever they are encountered because, unfortunately, they won't go away by themselves. The good news is, bias *can* be overcome through consciousness raising and education, as can be shown from other examples in our society. It is our challenge to counter inaccuracies and inequalities regarding adoption, knowing that only *we* care enough to do so.

And *how* can bias toward adoption be countered? In addition to the personal, face to face education that has been modeled in numerous vignettes in this book, there is another effective way to alert large numbers of people to the problem and to educate them. It is through the time-honored method of letter writing.

Since the media—screen, airwaves, and print—not only reflect but also reinforce public opinion, it is to people in the media that adoptive parents need to present the dual requests of accuracy and equality when the subject of adoption arises.

This has been my focus during the past four years, and I hope it will become yours. Sometimes a single letter has resulted in dramatic change on the part of some person in the media, a person who is, after all, a product of our society. Sometimes my friends and acquaintances across the country have combined efforts and mailed numbers of letters in an attempt to deal with a problem. Often positive results have been gained, but in every case, someone has been sensitized to the issue.

Here are some of the letters or excerpts of letters that I have written to producers, station managers, writers, and publishers during the past several years. You are invited to use these letters in part or in full to address a similar problem that arises in your area—an offer that renders a letter-writing task an easy one. View this chapter, then, as a call for action.

❖

John Ritter
c/o Susan Wilcox, Agent
PO Box 900
Beverly, Hills, CA 90213

Dear Mr. Ritter:

As three of us adoptive mothers approached the theater manager after our viewing of *Problem Child*, we were amazed to realize that he had not even thought about how anyone touched by adoption might react to the movie. I would like to tell you how we are reacting, and I would like to ask for your help.

The enclosed correspondence will tell you the depth of my concern, and it reflects the feelings of countless adoptive families across the nation. I do understand your intentions in this film. Junior is, after all, a wronged child, and the shallow adults (other than yourself) and children who surround him are way out of line.

Unfortunately, this won't matter to the nine-year-old who sees this film and comes out with negative attitudes regarding adoption and armed with taunts to throw at adopted children, whatever the intent of the movie.

Could I tell you, please, how hard we adoptive parents work to be sure our children are certain they are a "real" part of our families, that they are our "forever" children. Understandably, fear about this subject lurks not far below the surface in most adopted children. But the little girl in your film says, "He's not even a real kid. He's adopted." And Grandpa says, "I hope you kept the damn receipt. Get rid of him."

Could I tell you, please, how hard we adoptive parents work to be sure our children have positive feelings toward their birthparents, people who for any number of reasons felt they were unable to parent a child at that time, and so made a difficult but loving decision to allow their child to be adopted. This concept, as you can imagine, is related to a positive self-image in an adopted child. But Grandpa in your film says, "He has garbage blood. His parents probably met in the loony bin."

Could I ask you to consider for a moment, please, how our little child, our child whom my husband and I adopted, would feel if those lines were overheard?

If you can help us keep this film out of the home video market, a great deal of damage will be avoided.

Sincerely,
Linda Bothun

Bob Simonds, Producer
Universal Studios
1000 Universal Studio Plaza
Bldg 22
Orlando, FL 32819

Dear Bob:

In response to your kind phone call to me last evening, I'm writing on behalf of the thousands of adoptive parents who will be relieved and thankful to hear your assurances about *Problem Child II*, that this second film will contain no unkind references to adoption.

While your call contained wonderful news, there is no getting around the fact that *Problem Child I* shouldn't have happened at all. May I reiterate my suggestion ... that scripts be screened for hurtful statements or innuendo regarding adoption. Scripts could easily be read by a responsible adoption professional who could flag any concerns.

Again, I thank you for your call and for having made the effort to raise your sensitivities regarding adoption. I realize it would have been much easier to ignore my letter. I applaud your courage in admitting your error and apologizing for the hurt caused by the first film.

Most sincerely,
Linda Bothun

A Call to Action

Sam Simon, Producer
20th Century FOX TV
10201 West Pico Blvd.
Los Angeles, CA 90035

Dear Mr. Simon:

I am writing you as an adoptive parent who has grown weary of hearing slurs regarding adoption appear on prime time television and on children's programs.

The Thursday, February 21, 1991, showing of "The Simpsons" on FOX Channel 5 overstepped the bounds of decency in allowing Bart, unchecked, to call his father's half-brother a bastard, to name but one of my concerns about this program.

While we as adults can understand that the Simpson parents are too simple-minded to refute their son, children are not going to catch this subtlety. This is not the use of the term in order to be instructive, Archie Bunker style. This is a cruel use of such a term.

Thoughtful and decent references to adoption belong in television programming because adoption is a facet of life. The media are becoming more sensitive to terminology regarding adoption, The Washington Post, for instance, publishing a list of positive terminology it would use in the future. I wouldn't like to see FOX left behind in a world where bias toward adoption is no longer fashionable.

Sincerely,
Linda Bothun

Response: By letter, Mr. Simon assured that more care would be taken in the future with the subject of adoption.

A Call to Action

Letter to the Editor published in the June 15, 1992, *TIME*

Misleading Adoption Analogy

I was appalled by the lead paragraph of your article on the unified Germany [World, April 13]. In referring to the new Germany's resembling "a child of doubtful lineage adopted as an infant into a loving family" whose friends and neighbors are worried by the possibility "that evil genes may lurk beneath a well-mannered surface," you intended doubtlessly to create a vivid analogy. In fact, you leveled an unconscionable insult at the millions of people who are adopted. No statistics confirm the insinuation that adopted children are more likely to become societal problems than their biological counterparts. No statistics confirm the "bad seed" theory. If the thought lingers in the mind of the public, it is because of just such negative stereotyping as yours.

Linda Bothun

Michael E. Hill, Editor
"TV Week"
The Washington Post
1150 15th Street, NW
Washington, DC 20017

Dear Mr. Hill:

A paragraph in the October 6-12 issue of "TV Week" describing Tuesday night's production of "In the Heat of the Night" caught my attention. The description, a copy of which is enclosed, refers to a man as the "natural" father of a boy who, along with his father, was caught in a dramatic situation. My concern as I write you is not with the plot of this particular program but rather with the terminology you have chosen in your description.

The preferable words to describe this man would be "birthfather." "Natural father" is problematic in that it tends to suggest adoptive parents are the opposite ... "unnatural parents."

While the distinction may seem minor to you, it is of great import to children who were adopted. The bonding process between a child and his adoptive parents is essential, and for the child to read that someone else is his "natural parent" or his "real parent" (another favorite in the media) is confusing, to say the least. A child can understand that someone else gave birth to him but was unable to parent him, but exact descriptive words are a necessity.

The Washington Post published some months ago a list of updated terminology that would be used in the future. Among the terms, I was happy to see, was the substitution of "birthparent" for "natural parent" or "real parent." I am hoping this decision will be reflected in the *Post's* "TV Week" magazine as well.

Sincerely,
Linda Bothun

Response: A phone call from Mr. Hill alerting me to the fact that he had used the term "birthparent" in a subsequent article.

A Call to Action

Peggy Roberson
National Desk Editor
Hearst News Service
1701 Penna. Ave. NW - 6th Floor
Washington, DC 20006

Dear Ms. Roberson:

I appreciated your presentation at the conference ... last weekend. We
need to grapple with issues concerning adoption in the media, especially the issue of germaneness, with the help of experts like you.

I sat in the workshop trying to put into words, however, my concern
about your assertion that the adopted status of a child in a family is
indeed germane if, for instance, an Asian child who was adopted is
pictured with her Caucasian family. "The readers are curious," I understood you to say in justification.

I cite what I consider to be an analogy in a recent article about a knife
stabbing incident in one of our local high schools. It was not a school in
which there were advertised racial tensions, and I as a reader *was* curious. I read every word of the text and was, though, unable to
satisfy my curiosity. And that was as it should be and was the
result of deliberate editorial policy.

I understand the confusion about this issue because it has taken years
for those of us directly involved with adoption to articulate our concern.
It is very subtle, and in the case of your Asian child above, seems benign.

It may be, however, one of our key issues since it *is* so subtle. For what
we do, if we continue to point out the adopted status of a child unless *he*
claims the information is pertinent (e.g. - "I killed my adoptive parents

because I never fit into their family") is to perpetuate the thought that adoption is somehow literally newsworthy, that it is something other than what it really is: one of the ways of building a family.

I tread nervously here, realizing I can be construed as advocating mere political correctness. I think, however, that I am instead drawing attention to one of the more insidious ways that stereotyping of adopted persons is perpetuated. If it is allowed in the seemingly benign cases, it is allowed with Son of Sam. We become accustomed to it. We don't see the harm. And the stereotyping continues.

Perhaps the issue of germaneness would be unimportant if we were not, as a nation, trapped in the "Son of Sam" mentality. We are, however, and the only way to break it is, as with race, to formulate editorial policy which forbids it.

Actually, equality of treatment is all we ask. If the adopted status of a person is deemed routinely germane, then certainly the biological status of any person born to his family is routinely germane. If it is editorial policy that both adoption and biology are always included in *every* article, whether the article involves adopted persons or not, equality would be achieved and adoption put into perspective.

Mr. Barone, your fellow panelist, insisted our letters should consist of only four paragraphs. Thank you for bearing with me.

Sincerely,
Linda Bothun

A Call to Action

Station Manager
WIVB TV Broadcasting Station
2077 Elmwood Avenue
Buffalo, NY 14207

Dear Manager:

I am writing to thank you for the understanding [that a viewer and an assistant in your office] eventually reached ... in a telephone conversation ... on October 8.

[The viewer's] concern was with your reporting that day of the story of the seven-year-old autistic child who had evidently been abandoned by her mother at a neighborhood playground. The child, you reported, had been adopted. [The viewer] phoned to ask about the germaneness of that fact.

Adoptive parents are beginning to call to the attention of the media the many times reference is made to the adopted status of a child or person—when no reference is ever made to his counterpart's biological status. Have children born to their parents ever been abused or horribly treated? Equality would call for their method of joining their families, also, to always be reported. Asking for equality, or strict adherence to germaneness, is our request.

A fourteen-year-old ... perhaps said it best when we spoke this summer of articles about the New York serial killer, Joel Rifkin. His adopted status was reported, while the biological status of Jeffrey Dahmer and Ted Bundy were never mentioned. [The fourteen-year-old] found an analogy. "It's like what we talk about at school all the time. If the race of a criminal is reported, it's like saying everyone of that race is a criminal. Race shouldn't be mentioned unless it's important. Neither should adoption."

This is a fourteen-year-old's plea for germaneness. When [the viewer] used the same analogy, asking the assistant in your office why the race of the mother in question wasn't mentioned, your assistant was quick to see the point.

I am writing to request that you make it editorial policy to delete, as you do with race, the method by which a person entered his family unless it is germane (If this mother had said, "I abandoned her because I adopted her and therefore felt no responsibility for her," this would have been germane and should have been reported. Short of even a hint of such reasoning, adoption in not germane in this account.) Deliberate editorial policy such as this would help to remove hurtful stereotypes of adopted persons and adoptive families.

Thank you for considering the concern of this letter. If you would like to discuss the issue, I would be glad to speak with you.

Sincerely,
Linda Bothun

A Call to Action

The following was written because the broadcast was aired in some parts of the country at 8 a.m. when children could have access to it.

Infinity Broadcasting Co.
600 Madison Avenue
New York, NY 10022

Dear Sir:

Attacks on adults who can defend themselves or shrug off cruel humor are one thing. Attacks on children are another.

Howard Stern crossed a line of decency by his recently aired assertions that: adopted persons are generally "sick"; people adopt children only out of desperation; if a child is then born into an adoptive family, the adopted child is abandoned; only morons become pregnant at 14 and they leave the children feeling bad about themselves; if a child is born into an adoptive family, that biological child is loved more than the adopted child.

I assert there are lines that even Howard Stern won't cross. I have never heard him or any DJ or comic make malicious fun of children from divorced families. How cruel that would be since these children are often already erroneously blaming themselves for the divorce. Similarly, adopted children often erroneously blame themselves for the fact that their birthparents could not raise them. But somehow Howard Stern and you by association feel the fears of an adopted child can be publicly ridiculed.

Research shows that adopted children fare well in this world. They can be damaged by verbal attacks, of course, as can any child. I don't envy you your responsibility.

Sincerely,
Linda Bothun

Response: none

A Call to Action

M. D. Eisner, Chairman
Walt Disney Company
500 S. Buena Vista Street
Burbank, CA 91521

Dear Mr. Eisner:

"What's the worst thing Mom and Dad could do to us?" the teenager asked his sister after they had disobeyed their parents in an heroic effort to save the cheetah. "Well, they could put us up for adoption..." was the response in this otherwise lovely family movie.

I understood, of course, the spirit in which these words were said and know that you meant to harm. I feel, though, that this may be all the more reason to call to your attention the hurtfulness of such statements.

My husband and I sat behind the twelve nine-year-olds we had brought to see Walt Disney's *Cheetah And Friends* in celebration of our son's birthday. We watched two children stiffen when the above words were spoken, two of those twelve who were themselves adopted. We felt once again the unnecessary pain that is inflicted upon our children by thoughtless comments such as this.

This statement encourages the thought that an adopted status in a family is somehow second-class. It says you were probably adopted because you were in some way "bad." It says adoption is rejection rather than a difficult but loving decision made by someone not in a position to parent a child. It says adoption is a terrible fate, the worst in the world, evidently a fate worse than death. While we're not attempting to shield our children from every unpleasantry that may come along, this one could easily have been avoided. I ached not only for the two children

215

I've mentioned, but for their siblings who were born into their families and for whom such words are confusing, and for the rest of the children, all receiving a negative message about adoption.

Most people today are supportive of adoption and certainly wouldn't purposely negate it. And yet, very unfortunately and very often, some of the old biases and hurtful phrases slip into conversations of most people, and these words are very destructive to the self-image and the self-esteem of a child who has been adopted.

And so I'm sending this letter ... with a plea that you consider in the future the feelings of children who have been adopted. In fact, to address the issue in broader terms, since families are built in such diverse ways in today's times, I would suggest you have your manuscripts reviewed by a professional who is sensitive to the nuances of blended families.

So intense was my reaction and so intense has been the reaction of other adoptive parents, and in addition, non-adoptive parents who were embarrassed by these words, that I feel obliged to make my letter available to agency newsletters, parenting magazines, and movie and video reviewers, particularly those who reach family audiences.

I thank you now for your consideration of my concern. I know that you join me in wanting to encourage positive self-concepts for our children and for every child, a goal that will directly contribute to a healthier society.

Sincerely,
Linda Bothun

Response: Disney removed the offensive scene from copies of the film that were distributed to the home video market.

Acknowledgments

Scores of people have already heeded the call to action. I thank my coast-to-coast contacts, too numerous to name, through PAAM, the organization I co-founded with Kathy Rankin in 1991 to promote Positive Adoption Attitudes in the Media. I am particularly grateful to those dozens of people who have been diligent in bringing issues to my attention and who have contributed their time and effort in educating people in the media regarding the need for accuracy and equality where adoption is concerned.

I thank the countless persons who have helped me, formally or informally, to make this book possible, especially Dotty Young, Julie Bengtson, Mickey Finn, Joan Krinsly, Joan and Bob DiBianco, Kathy Neill, Patti Pucatch, Vivian Boul, Deirdre Radanovic, Jan Gonder, and Nancie Hummel Park.

I thank lastly those persons whose opinions I value and whom I was bold enough to ask, busy as they were, to read the manuscript of this book. Susan Freivalds, Kent Ravenscroft, Pat and Alan Pollock, and Robin Allen have my lasting gratitude.

❖

Swan Publications
P.O. Box 15293
Chevy Chase, MD 20825
202-244-9092

Number of
copies   Total

_____ *Dialogues About Adoption*, by Linda Bothun.
216 pp/paper ISBN 0-9619559-1-0.
$12.95 plus $2.00 postage and handling.   _____

_____ *When Friends Ask About Adoption*, by Linda Bothun.
88 pp/paper ISBN 0-9619559-0-2.
$4.95 plus $1.30 postage and handling.   _____

_____ *PAAM Newsletter*, editor Linda Bothun.
Annual subscription $24.00.   _____

                              Total enclosed   _____

Please send to:

Name _____
Street address_____
City _____State_____ Zip _____